STUDENTS
FOR A
DEMOCRATIC
SOCIETY

STUDENTS FOR A DEMOCRATIC SOCIETY

A GRAPHIC HISTORY

Written by **HARVEY PEKAR**

Art by **GARY DUMM**

Edited by **PAUL BUHLE**

A Novel Graphic from Hill and Wang

A division of Farrar, Straus and Giroux

New York

Hill and Wang
A division of Farrar, Straus and Giroux
18 West 18th Street, New York 10011

Printed in the United States of America
Published in 2008 by Hill and Wang
First paperback edition, 2009

The Library of Congress has cataloged the hardcover edition as follows:
Pekar, Harvey.
    Students for a Democratic Society : a graphic history / written by Harvey Pekar ; art by
Gary Dumm ; edited by Paul Buhle—1st ed.
        p.   cm.
    A history of the group Students for a Democratic Society told in graphic form.
    ISBN-13: 978-0-8090-9539-1 (hardcover : alk. paper)
    ISBN-10: 0-8090-9539-4 (hardcover : alk. paper)
    1. Students for a Democratic Society (U.S.)—History. 2. College students—United
States—Political activity—History. 3. New Left—United States—History. I. Dumm,
Gary. II. Buhle, Paul, 1944- III. Title.

LA229.P395 2008
378.1'981—dc22

                                                                                    2007040641

Paperback ISBN-13: 978-0-8090-8939-0
Paperback ISBN-10: 0-8090-8939-4

Designed by Laura Dumm • Lettering by Gary Dumm

www.fsgbooks.com

CONTENTS

INTRODUCTION

This is the story, in art-comic form, of Students for a Democratic Society's first life (1960–69), with a final few pages devoted to its surprising revival in high schools and on campuses across the United States during another failed war two generations later.

This comic version of social history provides an artistic reconstruction of the organization's rocketing rise and fall. It thus adds insight unbound by the limits of prose analysis. The first section of the book offers the reader a concise overview, told from the rebels' point of view but also from that of vernacular social critic Harvey Pekar, a college dropout up the road from Kent State in depressed Cleveland, Ohio. The second section of the book goes in a markedly different direction. The basic viewpoint is not greatly changed, but the camera or artist's brush is refocused on the deeply personal, the deeply local.

This book is, finally, a series of stories from the life of a generation, ending where SDS peaked, at around eighty to a hundred thousand activists and followers. So much had happened so quickly around them, it was no surprise that many young radicals and quite a few conservatives imagined American society to be on the verge of some vast transformation. A significant chunk of SDSers joined and in some cases actually organized the women's liberation movement, the gay and lesbian movements, the environmental movement, and so on. These causes, still far from won almost a half century later, had been essentially invisible before the era of SDS. It is difficult for today's young people to conceptualize a society at once so self-satisfied and so deep in social conservatism, race sentiment, homophobia, environmental indifference, and the assumptions of fixed roles of the sexes, and just as difficult to imagine that all these issues were tackled almost simultaneously, and very largely by the young themselves. As the stories in the next pages reveal, SDS proved itself far from perfect. But the momentum that it did so much to create, the experience gained by its activists, outgrew as well as outlived SDS.

The Vietnam War was, of course, the central political issue of Students for a Democratic Society, as inevitable as its locus on the nation's campuses. The mystery of the rebellion unraveled in this book is that SDS and all its energies never resembled the specter that so many in powerful places and in lonely living rooms feared and pondered. If, according to polls conducted among them, a large segment of the student population considered itself somehow "revolutionary" by the peak years of 1968–70, it was not in the name of any revolution that had existed or would exist, perhaps any that could exist. The sheer Americanness of the rebellious sentiment comes through so clearly in the following pages because—to oversimplify the phenomenon badly—it had cross-grained middle American suspicion of centralized authority with radical opposition to the Vietnam War effort. Despite their own uncertainties and wild rhetoric against "Amerikkka," SDSers further cross-grained distinctly American traditions of women's political self-emancipation with the new situation for young people created by the availability of birth control (and, for many, sub rosa abortions). SDS's followers, the great majority of whom never bothered to actually join the organization, for a little while did much to make marijuana and long hair the anti-uniform of the generation that urgently wanted another way of life, one more cooperative, freer, and (as corny as it sounds) more loving.

In our twenty-first century, the perspective has, of course, become very different. Not because the doddering radical veterans of that era have lived through so many years (and tears, and beers) and still remain part of the largest population bubble. Not because the structure of American society has changed in any fundamental way. Rather, it has to do with the sobering fact that just as the sixties generation is itself entering old age, its hard-won lessons seem to have reappeared. Today the Empire has badly overreached again. Our political elite is once again in disarray. The current Iraqi conflict, raising the voices of the powerful against each other as never since the sixties, exposes the flawed logic of Empire. However different the nation has become in forty years, creativity still arguably blossoms best among youth, those who have the least stake in the existing rules of society.

The reason that the 1960's have never quite gone out of common perspective is that the music, the cartoons and comics, the posters, the impulses, and the fears did not actually get old with the people who first lived them. The idea that any little group of saviors, self-avowed Weathermen or dogmatic Marxists, would lead America or the world into the promised land is over. Everyone in the Wal-Mart Nation knows better. But the crises didn't really go away, any more than did the urgent need and the simultaneous improbability of an inspired mass awakening to a better, more ecologically sound, more peaceful and cooperative, Age of Aquarius–like future.

—Paul Buhle and Harvey Pekar

STUDENTS
FOR A
DEMOCRATIC
SOCIETY

SECTION 1

SDS HIGHLIGHTS

STORY BY **HARVEY PEKAR**
ART BY **GARY DUMM**

UPTON SINCLAIR

SDS WAS THE LARGEST AND MOST POWERFUL **NEW LEFT** ORGANIZATION IN THE 1960'S. IT GREW OUT OF LID (LEAGUE FOR INDUSTRIAL DEMOCRACY), WHICH WAS FOUNDED IN **1905** BY INTELLECTUALS INCLUDING AUTHORS UPTON SINCLAIR AND JACK LONDON. IT WAS INITIALLY NAMED THE **INTERCOLLEGIATE SOCIALIST SOCIETY.**

JACK LONDON

LID ESTABLISHED **SLID** (THE **STUDENT LEAGUE FOR INDUSTRIAL DEMOCRACY**) IN THE 1930'S, AND SLID BECAME **STUDENTS FOR A DEMOCRATIC SOCIETY (SDS)** IN 1960. AL HABER, SDS'S FIRST PRESIDENT, WAS THE SON OF A MICHIGAN LABOR ARBITRATOR CLOSELY CONNECTED TO IMPORTANT LABOR LEADERS IN THAT STATE.

AL HABER

3

At first SDS, like LID, was set up as an avowedly **ANTICOMMUNIST**, **LIBERAL**, and **LEFTIST** organization. LID leaders grew alarmed that SDS members had some contact with individual **COMMUNISTS**, and, to punish them, **LOCKED THE DOOR** of the SDS office.

HABER, using knowledge gained in his high school **INDUSTRIAL ARTS** class, **PICKED THE LOCK** and **OPENED THE DOOR**. SDS became **INDEPENDENT** from LID after a few **UNEASY** years.

TOM HAYDEN

SDS's most **IMPORTANT DOCUMENT** was the **PORT HURON STATEMENT**, of **1962**, drafted at United Auto Workers summer camp in **PORT HURON, MICHIGAN**.

LID at first **ACCEPTED** the document, but **NOT TOO HAPPILY**. It had been drafted collectively, but the principal writer was **UNIVERSITY OF MICHIGAN** student **TOM HAYDEN**, the SDS president in **1962–63**. HAYDEN went on to become SDS's most **PROMINENT** figure.

THE
PORT HURON STATEMENT

...we seek the establishment of a democracy of individual participation governed by two central aims; that the individual share in those social decisions determining the quality and direction of his life; that society be organized to encourage independence in men and provide the media for their common participation...

Students for a Democratic Society

35¢

MANY OF THE SDSERS HAD WORKED IN THE CIVIL RIGHTS MOVEMENT AND SOUGHT TO EMULATE ITS GRASSROOTS ORIGINS, ITS FREEWHEELING PARTICIPATORY DEMOCRACY. SDS IDENTIFIED THE "MILITARY-INDUSTRIAL COMPLEX" AS A SOURCE OF THE NATION'S DISTORTED DEVELOPMENT, AND SOUGHT TO REPLACE, NOT MERELY REFORM, THIS CENTER OF ECONOMIC AND POLITICAL AUTHORITY.

IN THE EARLY 1960'S, SDS WAS ONE OF SEVERAL IMPORTANT NEW PROGRESSIVE MOVEMENTS, INCLUDING THE CIVIL RIGHTS GROUPS SNCC (STUDENT NONVIOLENT COORDINATING COMMITTEE) AND CORE (CONGRESS OF RACIAL EQUALITY) AND THE BERKELEY FREE SPEECH MOVEMENT. ALL THESE WERE MORE INFORMALLY RUN THAN THE OLD LEFT HAD EVER BEEN.

HABER EARLY ON TRIED TO FORGE COOPERATION BETWEEN THE STUDENT AND CIVIL RIGHTS MOVEMENTS. HAYDEN AND OTHER SDSERS RISKED THEIR LIVES IN THE SOUTH TO ADVANCE THE CIVIL RIGHTS CAUSE.

HABER ALSO DID HIS BEST TO PROMOTE UNDERSTANDING BETWEEN STUDENT ACTIVISTS AND LABOR. LABOR LEADERSHIP, GROWN DEEPLY BUREAUCRATIC AND CONSERVATIVE, DID NOT WARM TO THE STUDENT RADICALS.

IN ADDITION TO WORK IN THE **LABOR** AND **CIVIL RIGHTS** AREAS, **SDS** FORMED **ERAP** (ECONOMIC RESEARCH AND ACTION PROJECT), WHICH THEY USED TO TRY TO **ORGANIZE** IMPOVERISHED COMMUNITIES.

I GUESS WE HAVE **NO** ALTERNATIVE BUT A RENT STRIKE.

SDS WAS CONSISTENTLY **AGAINST** THE U.S. POLICY OF USING **WAR** TO FURTHER **NATIONAL** INTERESTS (AND **BUSINESS** INTERESTS). FROM THE MID-1960'S, **SDS** BEGAN TO **CALL** FOR DEMONSTRATIONS TO END THE **INVASION OF VIETNAM**.

THOUGH NOT MANY **REALIZED** IT AT THE TIME, **1960** WAS A GREAT YEAR TO BEGIN A RADICAL CAMPUS MOVEMENT. THE **NUMBER** OF STUDENTS ATTENDING **AMERICAN** COLLEGES AND UNIVERSITIES WAS **GROWING** RAPIDLY. MANY OF THE MORE **LIBERAL** WANTED TO GET INVOLVED IN THE **CIVIL RIGHTS** AND **ANTIWAR** MOVEMENTS. AND THEY WERE MORE AND MORE **SKEPTICAL** OF WHAT THE **ESTABLISHMENT** WAS **TELLING** THEM.

WHY, YOU **NEVER** HAD IT SO **GOOD**.

HABER FELT THE **SDS** MOVEMENT WAS EXCITING AND **PROMISING**. HIS INITIAL **STRATEGY** INVOLVED WORKING WITH OTHER LIBERAL OR RADICAL GROUPS, TO TIE THEM **TOGETHER** SO THAT JOINT ACTION, SUCH AS **PICKETING** INSTITUTIONS ENGAGED IN RACIAL DISCRIMINATION, WOULD BECOME SUCCESSFUL. **HABER** BELIEVED THAT **SDS** HAD TO BE **ACTIVE** IN THE GREATER **COMMUNITY** TO ACHIEVE ITS GOALS. HE APPEARED AT A **NATIONAL STUDENTS ASSOCIATION** CONVENTION IN **AUGUST**, SPEAKING TO POTENTIAL **RECRUITS**. ONLY A FEW YEARS LATER WAS IT REVEALED THAT **NSA'S** OFFICERS WERE BEING **PAID** BY THE **CENTRAL INTELLIGENCE AGENCY**.

...**HABER** BEGAN WORKING WITH **OTHER** LIBERAL GROUPS SUCH AS THE CAMPUS ARM OF THE **AMERICANS FOR DEMOCRATIC ACTION (ADA)**.

GRADUALLY **SDS** MEMBERSHIP ROSE TO **250**, AND **NEW** CHAPTERS WERE CREATED AT A FEW **COLLEGES** AND **UNIVERSITIES**.

HABER CREATED A CIVIL RIGHTS **NEWSLETTER** AND PLANNED FOR A CIVIL RIGHTS **CONFERENCE**. PEOPLE BEGAN TO **NOTICE** HIM.

AFTER HE SMOOTHED OUT SOME **DIFFICULTIES** WITH **LID** MEMBERS, WHO FEARED THAT HE WAS MOVING TOO **FAST**...

SDS PRESIDENT HABER WORKED OUT OF NEW YORK, BUT SOUGHT TO NETWORK ALL OVER THE COUNTRY. TOM HAYDEN WAS FIELD SECRETARY, WORKING IN ATLANTA, PARTICIPATING IN LOCAL CIVIL RIGHTS WORK, AND WAS OFTEN BEATEN AND JAILED.

DURING THE 1961–62 WINTER HOLIDAY BREAK, SDS HELD A SMALL CONFERENCE IN ANN ARBOR, MICHIGAN. PARTICIPATING MEMBERS COULD NOT AGREE ON MUCH, BUT THE MOOD PROVED HARMONIOUS, AND VALUABLE CONTACTS WERE MADE.

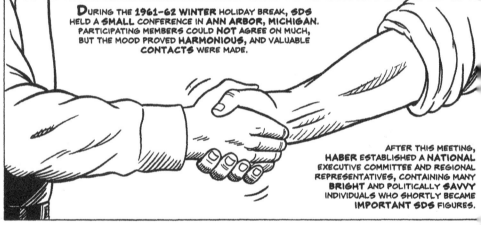

AFTER THIS MEETING, HABER ESTABLISHED A NATIONAL EXECUTIVE COMMITTEE AND REGIONAL REPRESENTATIVES, CONTAINING MANY BRIGHT AND POLITICALLY SAVVY INDIVIDUALS WHO SHORTLY BECAME IMPORTANT SDS FIGURES.

THE HIGHLIGHT OF THE SPRING–SUMMER OF 1962 WAS THE DRAFTING OF THE PORT HURON STATEMENT, WHICH NOT ONLY ANALYZED THE U.S. DOMESTIC AND FOREIGN POLICY ILLS BUT SHOWED HOW THEY WERE RELATED.

BECAUSE SDS WAS RELATIVELY MILD IN ITS CRITICISM OF COMMUNISM, COLD WAR HARDLINERS FROM LID THREATENED TO WITHDRAW SUPPORT FOR THE GROUP. AT A JULY 6, 1962, SHOWDOWN MEETING ON THE ISSUE...

UNITED FRONTISM IS A SLANDEROUS CHARGE. WE'RE NOT SUPPORTING THESE GROUPS BUT MERELY STATING OUR POSITION PROCEDURALLY.

NOTHING CONCLUSIVE WAS SETTLED THEN OR IN SUBSEQUENT MEETINGS. FOR THE TIME BEING, LID AND SDS WERE ABLE TO GET AROUND THEIR DIFFERENCES.

LOOKS LIKE THINGS HAVE GONE BACK TO NORMAL – FOR NOW.

SDS'S PORT HURON STATEMENT WAS A SMASH HIT WITH MANY YOUNG ACTIVISTS, HOWEVER, AND GAINED SDS CREDIBILITY.

I WENT OVER THE SDS'S PORT HURON STATEMENT IN DETAIL AND NOW FIND MYSELF ENTHUSIASTIC...TO THE POINT OF EFFERVESCING.

IN 1962 AND 1963 SDS WAS BESET BY ORGANIZATIONAL PROBLEMS THAT HAD NEVER BEEN SOLVED. MOST SDSERS WANTED A RELATIVELY DECENTRALIZED ORGANIZATION. DUE TO A LACK OF RESOURCES, THE NATIONAL OFFICE (N.O.) HAD RELATIVELY LITTLE CONTACT WITH THE LOCAL CHAPTERS ANYWAY; EACH CHAPTER WENT ITS OWN WAY. ACCORDING TO THE ULTRA-DEMOCRATIC CONSTITUTION, OFFICERS COULD NOT BE REELECTED. MANY TALENTED AND EXPERIENCED LEADERS SIMPLY DRIFTED AWAY.

WE HAVEN'T HEARD FROM THE NATIONAL OFFICE IN WEEKS. WE'VE GOT TO COORDINATE OUR ACTIVITIES BETTER.

THERE WAS **SOME** IMPORTANT ACTIVITY, HOWEVER. CONFERENCES WERE HELD ON THE **ROLE OF THE STUDENT** IN SOCIETY AND **"UNIVERSITY REFORM."** HERE SDSERS DISCUSSED WHAT HAPPENS WHEN A UNIVERSITY IS TAKEN OVER BY GOVERNMENT OR **CORPORATE** INTERESTS.

THE UNIVERSITY IS **SUPPOSED** TO BE WORKING **FOR US,** NOT **AGAINST US.**

IN JUNE 1963 "AMERICA AND THE NEW ERA" WAS **ISSUED** AS A DOCUMENT TO SUPPLEMENT **THE PORT HURON STATEMENT.**

IT NOTES THAT A **NEW ERA** IS UPON US, THE AMERICAN PEOPLE ARE **NOT** GETTING THE **ECONOMIC** SUPPORT THEY NEED FROM OUR GOVERNMENT, WHICH IS ALSO **NOT** DOING ENOUGH TO **COMBAT** RACISM.

HARVEY PEKAR

IN 1963, WITH THE HOPE OF BECOMING ONE WITH THE **POOR** PEOPLE, SDS BEGAN ITS **ERAP.** SMALL GROUPS OF **SDSERS** WERE **SENT** OUT TO VARIOUS CITIES TO **LIVE** IN IMPOVERISHED NEIGHBORHOODS, WHERE THEY WERE DETERMINED TO **POLITICIZE** AND EVEN **RADICALIZE** THEIR INHABITANTS.

THEY CLAIM WE'RE LIKE THE **RUSSIAN** STUDENT **NARODNIKS** OF THE 1860'S AND '70S. THEY TRIED TO LIFT THE POOR TOO, BUT THEIR EFFORTS PRETTY MUCH **FLOPPED.**

ACTUALLY, BY 1965, MOST OF THE SDS EFFORTS IN POOR NEIGHBORHOODS HELPED THE IMMEDIATE SITUATION OF THE POOR ONLY A LITTLE. THE RESIDENTS HAD DIFFERENT VALUES THAN THE MIDDLE-CLASS SDSERS AND WERE HARD TO ATTRACT AND ORGANIZE.

COMIN' TO THE MEETING TONIGHT?

I DON'T KNOW. I MIGHT HAVE TO GO SOMEWHERE ELSE.

AND YET ON A NATIONAL LEVEL SDS'S MEMBERSHIP INCREASED. STUDENTS HAD BEEN RADICALIZED BY THE CHURCH BOMBING IN BIRMINGHAM, THE KENNEDY ASSASSINATION, THE MURDERS OF SNCC WORKERS ANDREW GOODMAN, JAMES CHANEY, AND MICHAEL SCHWERNER, THE FAILURE OF THE MISSISSIPPI FREEDOM DEMOCRATIC PARTY TO BE RECOGNIZED IN THE 1964 DEMOCRATIC CONVENTION, AND THE BERKELEY UPRISING IN THE FREE SPEECH MOVEMENT.

DEMOCRATIC PARTY OFFICIAL

ALL WE CAN OFFER YOU IS TWO AT-LARGE DELEGATE SEATS.

WHAT? BUT WE MISSISSIPPIANS SUPPORT THE DEMOCRATIC PARTY.

THE SO-CALLED REGULAR DEMOCRATS ARE RACISTS.

THE MOST PRESTIGIOUS PROJECT, "N-CUP" (NEWARK COMMUNITY UNION PROJECT) IN NEWARK, NEW JERSEY, LASTED UNTIL 1967. MOST WERE SHORT-LIVED. ERAP WAS A VALUABLE LESSON TO SDS, HOWEVER, HUMBLING CERTAIN MEMBERS AND DISABUSING THEM OF SOME ROMANTIC NOTIONS THEY HAD ABOUT THE POOR.

WOW, I GOTTA ADMIT I DIDN'T KNOW WHAT I WAS GETTING INTO.

1965 WAS AN ACTION-FILLED YEAR FOR SDS. ON MARCH 19, IT LED A DEMONSTRATION IN DOWNTOWN MANHATTAN AGAINST THE CHASE NATIONAL BANK, WHICH HAD BEEN DOING BUSINESS WITH THE APARTHEID GOVERNMENT OF SOUTH AFRICA. ON MARCH 24 IT WAS INVOLVED IN A NEW KIND OF ACTIVITY INSPIRED BY THE CIVIL RIGHTS MOVEMENT: THE "TEACH-IN," FIRST HELD ON THE UNIVERSITY OF MICHIGAN CAMPUS IN ANN ARBOR.

11

AN EVEN BIGGER EVENT, ON APRIL 17, WAS THE SDS-SPONSORED DEMONSTRATION OF 25,000 AT THE WHITE HOUSE AGAINST THE VIETNAM WAR, THE BIGGEST ANTIWAR DEMONSTRATION TO DATE.

NO MORE WAR

OUT OF VIET NAM

PEAC NO

SDS AGAINST THE WAR

SDS PRESIDENT PAUL POTTER GAVE THE SPEECH OF THE DAY. THE EVENT WAS PUBLICIZED HEAVILY BY THE MEDIA AND LED TO ANOTHER UPSURGE IN SDS MEMBERSHIP.

WHAT KIND OF SYSTEM IS IT THAT JUSTIFIES THE UNITED STATES OR ANY COUNTRY SEIZING THE DESTINIES OF THE VIETNAMESE PEOPLE AND USING THEM CALLOUSLY FOR ITS OWN PURPOSE...WE MUST NAME THE SYSTEM!

AFTER THE DEMONSTRATION, THE SDS NATIONAL OFFICE MOVED FROM NEW YORK TO CHICAGO, PARTLY TO PUT SOME SPACE BETWEEN ITSELF AND LID OFFICIALS WHO STILL GAVE FUNDING BUT WERE INFURIATED THAT SDSERS CONTINUED TO APPEAR IN THE SAME DEMONSTRATIONS WITH ANYONE ELSE WHO JOINED, REFUSING TO BAR COMMUNISTS SPECIFICALLY.

THEY DIDN'T HAVE TO FIGHT COMMUNISTS IN THE '30S LIKE WE DID. THEY'RE TOLERATING TOTALITARIANISM.

SDS SET UP SHOP IN THE WOODLAWN GHETTO, JUST SOUTH OF THE UNIVERSITY OF CHICAGO.

WATCH IT, NOW, WATCH IT.

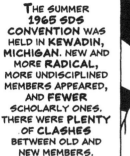

THE SUMMER 1965 SDS CONVENTION WAS HELD IN KEWADIN, MICHIGAN. NEW AND MORE **RADICAL**, MORE **UNDISCIPLINED** MEMBERS APPEARED, AND **FEWER** SCHOLARLY ONES. THERE WERE PLENTY OF **CLASHES** BETWEEN OLD AND NEW MEMBERS.

SDS IS SUPPOSED TO BE A **DEMOCRACY,** SO WHY DO WE **NEED** A **PRESIDENT** AND **NATIONAL OFFICE?**

SDS VETERAN **STEVE MAX** WASN'T HAPPY WITH THE NEW **BREED.**

THE **ROLE** OF THE **CHAIRMAN** VANISHED; AT **THIS** YEAR'S CONVENTION, FULL PLENARY SESSIONS OF **250** PEOPLE WERE PICKED BY MEMBERS AT **RANDOM** WITH **NO** REGARD TO **ABILITY**...SOME KEY VOTES WENT **UNCOUNTED.**

ATTEMPTS TO UPDATE **SDS'S** CURRENT POLITICAL POSITIONS WERE **THWARTED.**

ALL **OPPOSED.**

NAY,

NAY,

NAY,

NAY!

THE ELOQUENT **CARL OGLESBY** WAS ELECTED **SDS** PRESIDENT. AFTER THE **APRIL WHITE HOUSE** DEMONSTRATION, THE SOMEWHAT OLDER **OGLESBY** REMARKED:

STUDENTS! I HAD **NO** IDEA UNTIL **NOW** THAT **YOUNGER** PEOPLE - ANYONE - COULD **THINK** SO WELL.

THE CONVENTION **REMOVED** A CLAUSE BARRING MEMBERSHIP TO INDIVIDUAL **COMMUNISTS.** ENRAGED **LID** OLD–TIMERS CONSIDERED THIS PRACTICALLY THE **LAST** STRAW, BUT TO ORDINARY **SDSERS**, IT WAS NO **BIG DEAL.**

WE **SHOULD** HAVE DONE THIS YEARS AGO.

WHEN THE **KEWADIN** CONFERENCE CLOSED, NO ONE COULD BE **SURE** WHERE **SDS** STOOD ON SOME KEY **ISSUES**, INCLUDING WHETHER IT SHOULD TAKE A **STRONG** LEADERSHIP ROLE IN THE **ANTIWAR** MOVEMENT OR THE **NEW LEFT** IN GENERAL. FORMER PRESIDENT **TODD GITLIN** REMARKED LATER:

WHAT WE SURRENDERED **THEN** WAS THE **CHANCE** FOR AN ANTI–IMPERIALIST **PEACE** MOVEMENT.

THERE WAS ALSO CONTROVERSY ABOUT WHETHER TO **CONCENTRATE** SO MUCH ON **COLLEGE** STUDENTS OR **REACH** OUT TO THE **GREATER COMMUNITY.**

I WANT TO SEE US TAKE **SERIOUSLY** THE POSSIBILITY OF **RADICAL** WORKERS, SCIENTISTS, DOCTORS, CITY PLANNERS, ECONOMISTS, SOCIOLOGISTS, POETS, AND MOTHERS.

SOME COMMENTATORS HAVE THE **OPINION** THAT THE **KEWADIN** EVENTS WERE SORT OF A BEGINNING OF THE **END** FOR AN EARLY PHASE OF **SDS.** A YOUNGER, MORE ACTION–ORIENTED GROUP WAS TAKING OVER. AS IT DID, SOME OF THE MORE **EXPERIENCED** LEADERS DROPPED BACK OR DROPPED OUT OF THE ORGANIZATION.

WE DIDN'T HAVE **ENOUGH** OF OUR PEOPLE **THERE** BECAUSE MOST PEOPLE SAID "AW, **FUCK IT!**" OTHER KINDS OF PEOPLE GOT INTO THE N.O. AND COULDN'T **CONTROL** IT... FINALLY, THE THING GOT OUT OF HAND.

BUT WITHOUT EXPERIENCED STAFF, **SDS** WAS HARD PUT TO RUN AN ORGANIZATION. IN **JULY**, **SDS'S CHICAGO** PHONE WAS DISCONNECTED FOR **10 DAYS**; CONSISTENTLY IN NEED OF **MONEY, SDS** WAS FREQUENTLY FLAT **BROKE** AND IN A STATE OF **NEAR** COLLAPSE.

SOME OF THE **OLDER** MEMBERS HAD TO STEP IN TO **RESTORE** ORDER.

OKAY, WHERE DID YOU PUT THE **ACCOUNTS?**

UNCERTAIN HOW TO **ACT**, THE **SDS** NATIONAL OFFICE ISSUED A STATEMENT **CRITICAL** OF A PROPOSED **NATIONAL PEACE MARCH.**

PARTICIPATION IN THE **SYMBOLIC ASSEMBLY** SHOULD BE SERIOUSLY **QUESTIONED**, BECAUSE THE ASSEMBLY WILL **NOT** BE REAL. IT REPRESENTS **NO ONE** EXCEPT THOSE PARTICIPATING.

THERE WAS **NO** AGREEMENT ABOUT **ANTIWAR** ACTIVITIES. BUT A HOSTILE MEDIA AND RED-BAITING POLITICIANS VIRTUALLY MADE **SDS** INTO AN ANTIWAR MOVEMENT WITH CHARGES THAT **SDS** WAS PLANNING A MASSIVE **ANTIDRAFT** CAMPAIGN. **SDS** HAD NO CLEAR PLANS, BUT HEAVY LOCAL **SDS** PARTICIPATION IN THE **OCTOBER 15-16** TEACH-INS AND DEMONSTRATIONS IN **90** CITIES ACTIVATED **DOZENS** OF CHAPTERS AND BROUGHT IN **HUNDREDS** OF MEMBERS.

MEANWHILE, **SDS** AND **LID** HAD AGREED TO SEPARATE FORMALLY ON **OCTOBER 4, 1965.**

THEY'RE **SOFT** ON THOSE **VIETNAMESE REDS.** THEY WON'T GET ANOTHER **PENNY** FROM US.

A MARCH ON **THANKSGIVING** DAY BROUGHT **40,000** TO THE CAPITAL AND A NEAR-BREAK WITH THE "MODERATE," SEVERELY **ANTICOMMUNIST** PEACE ORGANIZATION **SANE.** NEAR THE END OF THE PROGRAM, **SDS** PRESIDENT **CARL OGLESBY** DELIVERED AN ELOQUENT SPEECH THAT GOT IMMEDIATE NATIONAL ATTENTION AND WIDE **PRAISE.** HE TALKED ABOUT MEMBERS OF THE **KENNEDY** AND **JOHNSON** ADMINISTRATIONS.

THEY ARE **NOT** MORAL MONSTERS, THEY ARE **ALL** HONORABLE MEN. THEY ARE ALL **LIBERALS.** BUT SO, I'M **SURE,** ARE MANY OF **US.**

OLGESBY'S SPEECH, NAMING THE IDEOLOGY OF "CORPORATE LIBERALISM" AS RESPONSIBLE FOR THE INVASION OF **VIETNAM,** SET OFF STILL ANOTHER BURST OF POPULARITY FOR **SDS** ON CAMPUS AND OFF.

THERE WAS **STILL** DISHARMONY IN **SDS** ABOUT PLANNING, ABOUT GOALS AND STRATEGIES. A NEW "RETHINKING CONFERENCE" WAS HELD AT **CHAMPAIGN-URBANA, ILLINOIS:** IT MADE **NO PROGRESS.**

JONATHAN EISEN WROTE IN "THE ACTIVIST" MAGAZINE:

It was a morass, a labyrinth, a marathon of procedural amendments, non sequiturs, soul searching and maneuvering...that went nowhere.

IN FEBRUARY 1966 SELECTIVE SERVICE HEAD **GENERAL LEWIS HERSHEY** ANNOUNCED THAT LOCAL DRAFT BOARDS COULD **INDUCT** COLLEGE STUDENTS WHO WERE IN THE **LOWER** PART, ACADEMICALLY, OF THEIR CLASSES. THE **2-C** CLASSIFICATION WOULD **NOT** PROTECT ALL COLLEGE STUDENTS FROM BEING **DRAFTED.** THIS SUDDEN THREAT SHOCKED THE **STUDENT** POPULATION.

GENERAL HERSHEY

NO 2-C!? &@#/☆?!

AFTER SOME UNCERTAINTY, SDS DECIDED TO HAVE CHAPTERS HAND OUT A **LEAFLET** OUTLINING THEIR POSITION **AGAINST** THE DRAFT. THIS TACTIC WAS A **FLOP.** FEW STUDENTS WERE PREPARED TO PUT THEMSELVES IN DANGER BY **RESISTING** THE DRAFT OPENLY.

SDSERS PRESSED THEIR **ANTIDRAFT** DECISION MORE VIGOROUSLY. BY **MAY 1966** DEMONSTRATIONS AND SIT-INS BY STUDENTS PROTESTING THE PARTICIPATION OF COLLEGES AND UNIVERSITIES WITH THE DRAFT **SWEPT** THE COUNTRY.

NO TO UNIVERSITY COMPLICITY WITH THE DRAFT

DURING THE UNPRECEDENTED SIT-IN AT THE ELITE **UNIVERSITY** OF **CHICAGO, SDS**ERS AND OTHER STUDENTS TOOK OVER THE ADMINISTRATION BUILDING FOR SEVERAL DAYS. HERE AND AT OTHER SIT-INS, STUDENTS DISCOVERED DAMNING **CONFIDENTIAL** DOCUMENTS **LINKING** THE UNIVERSITY ADMINISTRATIONS INTIMATELY TO THE MILITARY-INDUSTRIAL COMPLEX AND TO **CIA** MISDEEDS.

HMM. WELL, I'LL BE DARNED.

THESE SIT-INS, DEMONSTRATIONS, AND EXPOSED SECRETS RAISED **SUSPICION** AMONG STUDENTS AND FACULTY ABOUT THE VERY **PURPOSES** OF AMERICAN COLLEGES: WERE THEY **EDUCATING** YOUNG PEOPLE, OR WERE THEY **FEEDING** THE **EMPIRE?** THOUSANDS REGISTERED SHOCK AND UNEASE.

WHY, THOSE ROTTEN...

More and more "FREE" universities were set up over the next **COUPLE OF YEARS.**

THERE WILL BE **NO GRADES OR TESTS** IN **THIS CLASS.**

IN JANUARY 1966 SDS ESTABLISHED A WEEKLY NEWSPAPER, "**NEW LEFT NOTES,**" WHICH BECAME WIDELY READ BY OTHER YOUNG RADICALS. **EVERYONE** IN SDS HAD THE RIGHT TO **SUBMIT** ITEMS FOR PUBLICATION.

WHY IS THE TITLE **ALL** IN **SMALL** LETTERS?

THIS IS A MOVE-MENT, NOT SOME **MARXIST** PARTY, AND THAT'S THE **WAY WE WANT** IT.

left notes

NOT LONG AFTER, THE **PROGRESSIVE LABOR PARTY (PLP)**, A COM-MUNIST OFF-SPLIT FAC-TION SUPPORTING **MAO ZEDONG**, DISSOLVED ITS OWN YOUTH ORGANIZATION, THE **MAY 2ND MOVEMENT**, AND DIRECTED MEMBERS TO JOIN SDS, PLANNING TO **INFLUENCE** THE LARGER MOVEMENT AND TO **RECRUIT** MEMBERS FOR THEMSELVES.

SEE, **OUR** ANALYSIS **SHOWS...**

MEANWHILE, **SDS** WAS BEING MORE CLOSELY **WATCHED** BY A VARIETY OF GOVERNMENT AGENCIES INCLUDING THE FBI, WHO SENT **HUNDREDS** OF **SPIES** TO INFILTRATE THE ORGANIZATION.

J. EDGAR HOOVER

ARE **WE** COMMUNISTS? WE WOULD **NEVER** BE THAT CONSERVATIVE!

CARL OGLESBY

ONE OF THE MOST **MILITANT** ORGANIZATIONS NOW ENGAGED IN ACTIVITIES PROTESTING **U.S. FOREIGN POLICY** IS A STUDENT YOUTH GROUP CALLED **STUDENTS FOR A DEMOCRATIC SOCIETY.** COMMUNISTS ARE ACTIVELY PROMOTING AND PAR-TICIPATING IN THE ACTIVITIES OF THIS ORGANIZATION, WHICH IS SELF-DESCRIBED AS A GROUP OF LIBERALS AND **RADICALS.**

SDS FACED OTHER TROUBLES, TOO. SNCC, A **MAJOR** CIVIL RIGHTS GROUP OF YOUNG PEOPLE, ANNOUNCED IT HAD BECOME AN **ALL-BLACK** MOVEMENT, SEPARATING ITSELF FROM **WHITE** LIBERAL AND RADICAL ORGANIZATIONS. THIS MOVE WAS SEEN AT THE TIME AS A HEAVY **BLOW** TO SDS, WHICH HAD VIEWED ITSELF AS A **PARTNER** TO SNCC.

WE **FEEL** LIKE WE SHOULD **DO** IT BY **OURSELVES.**

In some ways, SDS adapted remarkably fast to the changing **moods** on college campuses. By the time of SDS's national convention in **August 1966** at a church camp in **Clear Lake, Iowa**, it had a large number of new members from the midwestern plains states and the southwest, especially **Texas**. These new members advocated a **greater** degree of decentralization, even though SDS was **already** decentralized.

I'M FROM **AUSTIN, TEXAS**, AND I **DON'T** AGREE WITH TOP-DOWN POLITICS.

The new SDS vice president, **Carl Davidson**, came up with the intriguing concept of **"student syndicalism,"** with the **universities** as factories and **students** as the working people struggling for control.

OUR EDUCATIONAL INSTITUTIONS ARE **CORPORATIONS** AND **KNOWLEDGE FACTORIES**.

Davidson urged a **new** emphasis on the strategic importance of SDS building **chapters** by organizing the **students** to demand more democracy and transparency in colleges and universities.

SEE, IF STUDENTS COULD **CONTROL** THEIR EDUCATION...

National secretary **Greg Calvert** supported **Davidson's** plan and philosophized about its **significance**.

IT **MEANS** THAT WE ARE, AS WE HAVE OFTEN SAID, DEDICATED TO THE **BUILDING** OF TRULY RADICAL CONSTITUENCIES IN THIS COUNTRY, **STARTING** WITH WHERE WE ARE.

THE UPSURGE IN **SDS** ACTIVITY DURING THE **FALL OF 1966** FOCUSED MORE **PRESSURE** ON CAMPUS ADMINISTRATIONS TO ADMIT TO AND ABANDON THE **CONNECTIONS** BETWEEN THE UNIVERSITIES, CORPORATIONS, AND THE MILITARY.

A HUGE STUDENT STRIKE AT BERKELEY, SPARKED BY NAVY **RECRUITING** ON CAMPUS, WAS LED BY THE **VIETNAM DAY COMMITTEE (VDC).** MANY LOCAL **SDSERS** TOOK PART.

GENERAL, ALLOW ME TO **INTRODUCE** OUR COLLEGE PRESIDENT.

BOYCOTT YOUR CLASSES!!

SECRETARY OF DEFENSE ROBERT MCNAMARA MADE AN APPEARANCE AT **HARVARD** AND WAS **HECKLED,** THEN TRAPPED IN HIS LIMOUSINE, BY **SDSERS** AND OTHER STUDENTS. A POLICE GUARD WAS **NEEDED** TO TAKE HIM OFF CAMPUS.

McNAMARA

VROOOM

CALVERT HAD BY THIS TIME BECOME THE **KEY** FIGURE AT THE **CHICAGO** OFFICE AND, FOR A CHANGE, GOT THINGS DONE **SMOOTHLY.** HE RAILED SARCASTICALLY **AGAINST** THOSE WHO WANTED TO DECENTRALIZE **SDS** EVEN **MORE.**

> MAYBE WE OUGHT TO **REFUSE** TO BE A **NATIONAL** ORGANIZATION AND DECIDE THAT THE ONLY **REAL** PROBLEMS ARE **NEIGHBORHOOD** PROBLEMS.

THERE WERE DISCUSSIONS ABOUT ADOPTING A NEW **IDEOLOGY** REFLECTING THE **CHANGING** REALITIES OF **AMERICAN** LIFE.

> SOME OF US IN **SDS** MUST BEGIN TO EXPLORE AND **TALK** WITH MEMBERS ABOUT WHAT WE'RE **DOING,** WHAT IS OUR THEORY. THE **OLD** IDEAS DON'T MAKE **SENSE** ANYMORE.

A NEW **ANTIDRAFT** STRATEGY WAS ALSO BADLY **NEEDED.** OTHER GROUPS HAD COME UP WITH SOME **CREATIVE** WAYS TO RESIST. **SDS** WORKED TO CATCH UP.

> SURE, WE'RE WILLING TO **COOPERATE.** WHAT SHOULD WE DO?

SDS SOON CAME UP WITH THE IDEA OF A NATIONAL **DRAFT-RESISTANCE** PROGRAM.

THE **DRAFT**

NO MORE WAR

SDS HAS MOVED FROM PROTEST TO **RESISTANCE.**

21

IN FEBRUARY 1967 CALVERT MADE A **SPEECH** THAT ILLUSTRATED **SDS'S** RADICALIZATION.

SDS WAS MOVING TOWARD A **NEW** KIND OF **RADICAL** POSITION.

RADICAL OR **REVOLUTIONARY** CONSCIOUSNESS...IS THE **PERCEPTION** OF ONESELF AS **UNFREE,** AS OPPRESSED.

OUR PRIMARY TASK AT THIS STAGE OF DEVELOPMENT IS THE **ENCOURAGEMENT** OR BUILDING OF **REVOLUTIONARY** CONSCIOUSNESS.

IN SPRING 1967 STRONG **DRAFT-RESISTANCE** GROUPS EMERGED AT SEVERAL **UNIVERSITIES.** AND **HUNDREDS** OF INDIVIDUAL MEN **PLEDGED** TO REFUSE TO SERVE IN **VIETNAM.**

ANTIDRAFT BUTTONS

MY LIFE, YOU DON'T

NOT WITH MY LIFE, YOU DON'T

NOT WITH MY LIFE, YOU DON'T

ON APRIL 15, 1967, THERE WAS AN SDS-SPONSORED MASS DRAFT-CARD BURNING IN NEW YORK.

"THE NEW YORK TIMES'S" TOM WICKER WROTE:

If the Johnson administration had to prosecute 100,000 Americans...it would then be faced, not with dissent, but with civil disobedience on a scale amounting to revolt.

LARGE DEMONSTRATIONS WERE HELD AT CORNELL, PENN STATE, WISCONSIN, COLUMBIA, AND THE NEW SCHOOL FOR SOCIAL RESEARCH.

GEE, MAYBE A REVOLUTION IS POSSIBLE.

STILL MORE INSTANCES OF UNIVERSITY, BIG BUSINESS, AND MILITARY COLLUSION WERE BEING UNCOVERED.

WALL STREET JOURNAL

CAN THIS BE TRUE???

"RAMPARTS" MAGAZINE BROKE THE SHOCKING NEWS THAT THE NATIONAL STUDENT ASSOCIATION AND SOME OF THE MOST INFLUENTIAL ANTI-COMMUNIST LIBERAL MAGAZINES, LIKE THE "PARTISAN REVIEW" AND THE "NEW LEADER," WERE BEING SECRETLY FUNDED BY THE CIA, WHICH ALSO PAID FOR LAVISH CONFERENCES FOR "PATRIOTIC" LIBERAL INTELLECTUALS LIKE ARTHUR SCHLESINGER, JR.

MAN, WHAT COULD YOU EXPECT FROM THOSE BIG-SHOT LIBERALS? BUT I THOUGHT AT LEAST THE NSA WAS CLEAN.

THE BIGGER PLANS OF THE CIA AND FBI HAVE NOW BEEN EXPOSED: THEY WANT TO REPLACE SDS CHAPTERS WITH CAMPUS-BASED "MODERATE" GROUPS, AND REPLACE ANTIWAR BLACK LEADERS LIKE MARTIN LUTHER KING, JR., WITH SUPPORTERS OF THE WAR. THEY WON'T SUCCEED.

THE SPRING MOBILIZATION OF THE **COMMITTEE TO END THE WAR IN VIETNAM (CEWV)** BROUGHT TOGETHER 300,000 PEOPLE IN A DEMONSTRATION IN **WASHINGTON, DC.** SDS DID **NOT** INITIALLY PARTICIPATE, SAYING:

> THEY **TOLD** US, "**DON'T** MOBILIZE; ORGANIZE." BUT A LOT OF ACTIVISTS ARE **GOING** TO **WASHINGTON**.

AN INCREASING NUMBER OF **AMERICANS,** NOT ONLY **SDSERS** AND NOT ONLY YOUNG PEOPLE, BEGAN TO SEE MASS MARCHES AS **FUTILE.**

> SEEMS LIKE WE'VE HAD A MILLION OF THESE **MARCHES** AND IT **DOESN'T** SEEM TO INFLUENCE THE GOVERNMENT A **BIT.**

SDS SOUGHT NEW IDEAS TO **PREPARE** FOR A REVOLUTIONARY CHANGE IN **AMERICAN** SOCIETY. IN **NEW YORK**, THREE SUPER-BRIGHT STUDENTS (**BOB GOTTLIEB, GERRY TENNEY,** AND **DAVE GILBERT**) BEGAN TO WRITE UP A LONG-TERM ANALYSIS STRATEGY.

> THESE PEOPLE HAVE **HIT** ON SOMETHING WE CAN USE.

new left no

IN THE PAPER (CALLED WITH INTENTIONAL IRONY "**THE PORT AUTHORITY STATEMENT,**" BECAUSE IT WAS WRITTEN IN **MANHATTAN,** NOT **PORT HURON, MICHIGAN**), THE AUTHORS POINTED TO THE SUSTAINED GROWTH OF A NEW **WORKING CLASS** CONSISTING OF WELL-EDUCATED YOUNG TECHNOCRATS, BORED AND ALIENATED WITH THEIR **JOBS.**

> WHEN THE NEW WORKERS **REALIZE** THE **POWER** THEY HAVE, THEY WILL **CONCLUDE** THAT THEY CAN USE IT "**AS A FORCE** FOR SOCIAL CHANGE." STUDENTS CAN **START** TO MAKE AN **IMPACT** ON SOCIETY.

24

CALVERT WRITES A NOTE TO HIMSELF, SAYING:

WE CAN SEE BETTER **NOW** WHAT A **MISTAKE** IT WAS TO **ASSUME** THAT THE **ONLY** RADICAL ROLE THAT STUDENTS COULD **PLAY** WOULD BE AS ORGANIZERS OF **OTHER** CLASSES.

BUT JUST AS **SDSERS** BEGAN TO CONSIDER HOW THESE "TECHNOCRATS," OR TECHNOLOGY WORKERS, MIGHT BE THE VANGUARD OF A GREAT **CHANGE**, THEIR ATTENTION WAS **DIVERTED** BY THE ASSASSINATION OF **DR. MARTIN LUTHER KING, JR.**, AND A SERIES OF BLACK URBAN **REVOLTS** IN MANY CITIES.

BURN, BABY, BURN!

WHAT'S THE **POINT OF THEORY?** THE **REVOLUTION** IS IN THE **STREETS!**

BLACK REVOLT WAS MIRRORED BY STIRRINGS OF **WOMEN'S LIBERATION.** TEMPORARY NATIONAL SECRETARY **JANE ADAMS,** THE FIRST **WOMAN** TO OCCUPY A **HIGH POSITION** IN THE NATIONAL OFFICE, HAD FOUGHT AGAINST **SEX DISCRIMINATION** SINCE HER **CIVIL RIGHTS** DAYS. SDS DEALT WITH THIS PROBLEM **EARLIER** THAN MOST GROUPS IN THE **NEW LEFT** AND HAD MANY WOMEN AS **LOCAL** LEADERS, BUT MANY SDS WOMEN ALSO CONSIDERED THE **OFFICIAL** RESPONSE HALF-HEARTED AT BEST. THE WAR AND THE THREAT OF THE DRAFT REINFORCED THE **EMPHASIS** ON MALE STUDENTS.

JANE ADAMS

A YEAR EARLIER, AT THE **SDS** CONVENTION OF 1967 IN **EAST LANSING, MICHIGAN,** A **SPLIT** DEVELOPED BETWEEN MANY **CHAPTERS** AND THE MORE RADICAL (OR IDEOLOGICAL) **NATIONAL OFFICE.** MANY OF THE **SDSERS** AT THE LOCAL LEVEL WERE STILL BASICALLY **LIBERAL** AND UNCERTAIN ABOUT WHAT THE N.O. WAS DOING.

I WANTED TO ASK, ARE WE FOR USING **VIOLENCE?** AND IF SO, UNDER **WHAT** CONDITIONS?

AGREEMENT BETWEEN DIFFERENT GROUPS WAS HARD TO **ACHIEVE**, ALTHOUGH THEY DID COME TO SOME AGREEMENT OVER **TACTICS** IN OPPOSITION TO THE **WAR** AND THE **DRAFT**.

WE REALLY **HAVEN'T** GOT A **SOLID** PROGRAM FOR THE **NEXT** YEAR.

YEAH, WHICH **WAY** WILL WE **GO**?

MEANWHILE, A PLAN WAS ADOPTED TO DISTRIBUTE POWER MORE **EQUALLY** WITHIN THE NATIONAL OFFICE, PROVIDING **LOCAL** MEMBERS **MORE** INPUT. BUT AS THE DECENTRALIZED **GROWTH** OF CHAPTERS **CONTINUED** WITH LESS AND LESS CONTACT FROM THE **NATIONAL** OFFICE, **POWER** FELL INTO THE HANDS OF THE NATIONAL SECRETARY.

THE INEXPERIENCED **MIKE SPIEGEL** WAS ELECTED NATIONAL SECRETARY, **ROBERT PARDUN** THE EDUCATION SECRETARY, **CARL DAVIDSON**, INTERORGANIZATIONAL SECRETARY. **PARDUN**, MOST **EFFECTIVE** ON THE ROAD, TURNED OUT TO BE A BETTER **ORGANIZER** THAN ADMINISTRATOR. **DAVIDSON** FOUND HIMSELF IN A JOB THAT DID **NOT** MAKE FULL USE OF HIS ABILITIES AS **ORGANIZER**.

SPIEGEL

PARDUN

DAVIDSON

NEVERTHELESS, 1967 WAS AN ACTION-FILLED YEAR. **SDS** JUMPED INTO A NUMBER OF **FIGHTS** AND BECAUSE IT CONTINUED TO BE **ADMIRED** (OR HATED) AND TO GROW, IN **OCTOBER** 1967 CONFRONTATIONS BETWEEN CAMPUS OR LOCAL POLICE AND STUDENTS **ESCALATED**. IN SOME PLACES, **DOW CHEMICAL** (MAKERS OF **NAPALM**) HAD TO MEET **POTENTIAL EMPLOYEES** OFF CAMPUS, IN SECRET.

DOW

LIKEWISE DURING A **BERKELEY** UPRISING, CAMPUS DEMONSTRATORS USED HIT-AND-RUN TACTICS TO **THWART** SAFETY OFFICERS — THEY AND OTHER COLLEGE DEMONSTRATORS WERE NO LONGER **PASSIVELY** ACCEPTING BEATINGS.

IN NEW YORK, SEC. OF STATE DEAN **RUSK** WAS PICKETED BY PEOPLE WHO **THREW** BAGS OF PAINT AND COW'S BLOOD AND TRASH AT THE **RUSK** PARTY. SDS WAS STARTING TO TAKE THE **OFFENSIVE.**

ABOUT **60%** OF THE LARGE UNIVERSITIES WERE **HIT** BY PROTESTS, WHILE **106** REPORTED **ANTIRECRUITER** DEMONSTRATIONS IN THE **FALL.**

THESE DEMONSTRATIONS OFTEN **STARTED** OFF WITH **PEACEFUL** SIT-INS. WHEN PROTESTERS WERE **ATTACKED** BY POLICE, THEY WERE **SURROUNDED** BY CROWDS OF STUDENTS.

ON OCTOBER 21, 100,000 PEOPLE DEMONSTRATED **AGAINST** THE WAR AT THE **PENTAGON.** THEY ACTUALLY **BROKE** THROUGH GUARDS' LINES AND SPENT THE NIGHT ON THE GRASS.

AFTER THE **PENTAGON** DISRUPTION **CARL DAVIDSON** CAME UP WITH HIS **"TOWARD INSTITUTION RESISTANCE"** POSITION PAPER, CALLING FOR THE DISRUPTION, DISLOCATION, AND DESTRUCTION OF THE MILITARY'S **ACCESS** TO **MANPOWER**.

YEE-OoOWW!

OLD-FASHIONED "HOT FOOT"

SOME IN THE NATIONAL OFFICE **IMAGINED** A **REVOLUTION** ON THE HORIZON. STUDENTS AS A GROUP, INCLUDING LOCAL **SDSERS**, NOW DIDN'T SEEM **RADICAL** ENOUGH. THE IDEA OF THE **"NEW WORKING CLASS"** WAS TOO VAGUE AND DISTANT. THEY URGED **SUPPORT** OF GHETTO **UPRISINGS** AND ACTION BY THE **POOR** WHO WERE WILLING TO RISE UP **AGAINST** THE SYSTEM.

WHAT CAN STUDENTS DO? ORGANIZING **STRUGGLES** OVER DORMITORY RULES SEEMS **FRIVOLOUS** WHEN COMPARED TO THE GHETTO **REBELLIONS**.

AT THE **CHAPTER** LEVEL, MOST SDSERS WERE OPPOSED TO **VIOLENCE** AND FELT THEY WERE BEING **ABANDONED** BY THEIR **NATIONAL SDS** LEADERS.

MAN, THE N.O. DOESN'T ASK US **ANYTHING**. THEY **GO** AHEAD AND DO WHAT **THEY** WANT.

A **DEBATE** DEVELOPED OVER HOW TO CONCENTRATE SDS'S **EFFORTS** – ON **EITHER** BASE BUILDING OR **CONFRONTATION**.

YOU **THINK** THE REVOLUTION'S RIGHT **AROUND** THE CORNER, BUT WE NEED **MORE** PEOPLE, MORE **CLASSES** OF PEOPLE **WITH** US.

IRONICALLY THE N.O. LEADERS WERE PRESSING FAR HARDER FOR AN IMMINENT REVOLUTION THAN THE HARD-LINE **MARXIST PLERS,** WHO THOUGHT THEY WERE **MOVING TOO FAST.**

THE WORKING CLASS **ISN'T** BEHIND US YET; WE CAN'T AFFORD TO **ALIENATE** THEM WITH STREET DEMONSTRATIONS AND **LOOSE TALK.**

IN THE **DECEMBER 1967** NATIONAL COUNCIL MEETING, THE N.O. PROGRAM OF **"TEN DAYS TO SHAKE THE EMPIRE"** (PLANNED FOR APRIL) WAS TURNED DOWN BY A **COMBINATION** OF PL SUPPORTERS AND OTHER CHAPTER **ACTIVISTS.**

NAY! NAY! NAY! NAY! NAY! NAY! NAY!

THE **NAYS** HAVE IT.

NAY! NAY! NAY! NAY!

WHEN BERNARDINE DOHRN, A YOUNG LAWYER, JOINED **SDS** SHE WAS A **LIBERAL.** SOON SHE BECAME **RADICALIZED.** A FRIEND TALKS ABOUT HER:

WE STARTED **RIPPING** SIGNS AND THEN SOME KIDS **TRASHED** A **JEWELRY** STORE. BERNARDINE REALLY **DUG** IT...BUT AFTERWARD WE HAD A LONG **TALK** ABOUT **URBAN GUERRILLA** WARFARE AND WHAT **HAD TO BE DONE** NOW – BY ANY MEANS NECESSARY.

B**©©©**OM!

FROM **JANUARY** TO MAY **1968** THERE WERE TEN INCIDENTS OF **BOMBING** AND **BURNING** OF UNIVERSITY BUILDINGS, THE **FIRST** TIME **AMERICAN** STUDENTS HAD USED THESE **TACTICS.**

DAVIDSON AND **SDSERS** DISAPPROVED OF THE "**LEFT** ADVENTURERS'" VIOLENCE, BUT THE ORGANIZATION SEEMED TO BE **HEADED** IN THAT **DIRECTION.**

THE **CRAZIES,** I CALL 'EM!

THERE REALLY WERE **TEN DAYS** OF RESISTANCE THAT **SPRING.** RALLIES, MARCHES, AND SIT-INS WERE HELD IN AT LEAST **50 COLLEGES,** ENDING IN A **ONE-DAY** STUDENT STRIKE ON **APRIL 26,** WITH **THOUSANDS** OF LOCAL SDSERS PARTICIPATING. THE N.O. STAYED **CLEAR** OF ANY CLAIM TO **LEADING** THESE EVENTS.

U.S. OUT OF VIET-NAM

NO MORE WAR

MARCH FOR PEACE

END THE WAR NOW

THE MOST FAMOUS STUDENT TAKEOVER OF **BUILDINGS** WAS LED BY MARK RUDD AT **COLUMBIA** UNIVERSITY.

RUDD

THE POLICE **ENDED** THE **COLUMBIA** **OCCUPATION** AFTER ABOUT A **WEEK,** BUT AFTER STUDENTS WERE CHASED **OUT** OF THE **BUILDINGS** THEY MOUNTED A **SUCCESSFUL** **STRIKE.**

STRIKE

31

LIBERAL STUDENTS PROVED TO BE THE VAST MAJORITY OF THE STRIKERS, AND SDS HAD SUCCEEDED IN UNITING THEM. COLUMBIA ADMINISTRATORS CAPITULATED TO MOST OF THEIR DEMANDS.

THE COLUMBIA REVOLT SET OFF OTHERS IN COLLEGES ACROSS THE COUNTRY, MORE THAN EVER BEFORE.

COLUMBIA BERKELEY MADISON TULANE CHICAGO

SDS BENEFITED GREATLY IN INCREASED MEMBERSHIP AND DONATIONS SPURRED BY THE COLUMBIA STRIKE.

MORE THAN ANY OTHER EVENT IN OUR RECENT POLITICAL PAST, COLUMBIA HAS SUCCESSFULLY SUMMED UP AND EXPRESSED THE BEST ASPECTS OF THE MAIN THRUST OF OUR NATIONAL POLITICAL EFFORTS.

AT THE TIME OF ITS SUMMER 1968 CONVENTION, AN SDS STATEMENT ARGUED, "OUR MOVEMENT IS AN ELEMENT OF THE REVOLUTIONARY VANGUARD PAINFULLY FORMING FROM THE INNARDS OF AMERICA."

DO YOU BELIEVE THIS?

I DUNNO, WHO ELSE HAS GOTTEN AS FAR AS THEY HAVE?

SURVEYS SHOWED **HUNDREDS** OF **THOUSANDS**, MAYBE OVER A **MILLION**, COLLEGE STUDENTS REGARDED THEMSELVES AS **REVOLUTIONARIES**, A LARGE NUMBER OF THEM SYMPATHETIC TO **SDS**.

WHADDA YA **THINK** OF THAT?

MAYBE IT'S **TRUE**, BUT THEY'RE **NOT** ORGANIZED AND THEY HAVE A LOT OF **DIFFERENT** CONCEPTS OF **WHAT A REVOLUTIONARY** IS.

SDSER BOB PARDUN COMMENTED:

WHAT IT CAME TO **THAT YEAR** WAS THAT PEOPLE CONCLUDED THAT THE **ONLY** WAY TO **STOP THE WAR** WAS TO MAKE A REVOLUTION AND THE ONLY WAY TO STOP **RACISM** WAS MAKE A REVOLUTION.

WHAT WE OUGHT TO **DO** IS BUILD REVOLUTIONARY **GROUPS** IN BIG CITIES THAT **APPEAL** TO YOUNG PROFESSIONALS, HIGH SCHOOL KIDS, AS WELL AS **COLLEGE STUDENTS**.

JAIL BREAK!

BUT PL SUPPORTERS RESOLVED TO THWART **SDS** REGULARS AT **EVERY** TURN, MAKING **PROGRESS** DIFFICULT. THE **PLP** HAD ESPECIALLY SIGNIFICANT **SUPPORT** AT **CONVENTIONS**, SUPPORT THAT THEY HAD **CAREFULLY** ARRANGED.

WHERE IS THE **JUSTIFICATION** BASED ON **CLASS ANALYSIS** TO TAKE SUCH **MEASURES**?

33

LOSING PATIENCE, MORE AND MORE **SDSERS** URGED KICKING THE **PLERS** OUT OF THE ORGANIZATION. BUT **SDS** HAD PRIDED ITSELF ON ITS **NONEXCLUSIONARY** STAND, AND NOTHING LIKE THIS **CHALLENGE** HAD EVER HAPPENED.

IT'S SIMPLY NOT **PRINCIPLED** TO MOVE INTO SDS IN ORDER TO **RECRUIT** MEMBERS FOR **ANOTHER** PARTY.

BUT **WHAT** DO WE DO ABOUT THEM?

THE REGULARS **SUCCEEDED** IN ELECTING **TWO** CANDIDATES TO LEAD THE ORGANIZATION IN **1968**, **MIKE KLONSKY**, NATIONAL SECRETARY, AND **BERNARDINE DOHRN**, INTERORGANIZATIONAL SECRETARY. BOTH WERE AVOWEDLY **ANTI-PL**. FRED GORDON, PL SUPPORTER, WON THE POST OF EDUCATIONAL SECRETARY BY **ONE** VOTE.

WE ARE **NOT** GOING TO PUT UP WITH ANY **CRAP** FROM **THEM**.

MIKE KLONSKY

BERNARDINE DOHRN

THEN THE **SPOTLIGHT** TURNED TO THE **1968** DEMOCRATIC CONVENTION IN **CHICAGO**. **SDS** WAS AGAINST **ALL** THE NOMINEES AND, WITH A BUNCH OF OTHER GROUPS AND INDIVIDUALS, DENOUNCED THE CONVENTION AS A **FRAUD**.

THOSE OF **US** WHO HAVE BEEN IN THE **STREETS** FOR THE PAST **FIVE** DAYS DON'T GIVE A **FLYING FUCK** ABOUT GENE McCARTHY. THE **MACHINE** RUNS THE PARTY ANYWAY.

ELECT

McCARTHY

THE CRIMINAL **BRUTALITY** EMPLOYED BY THE **CHICAGO** POLICE TO BREAK UP THE DEMONSTRATIONS WAS **SEEN** BY EVERYONE ON **TELEVISION**. DEMONSTRATORS ALSO GOT LOCAL **SUPPORT** FROM A GROUP OF YOUNG PEOPLE WHO WERE **NOT** STUDENTS.

THE **WHOLE WORLD** IS **WATCHING!**

THAT FALL **SDS** GOT **NEW** MEMBERS AT AN **UNPRECEDENTED** RATE. **SDS** PEOPLE COULDN'T KEEP TRACK.

AT THE NATIONAL COUNCIL IN **OCTOBER**, **SDS** REGULARS PUT DOWN PLP'S PROPOSAL TO FOCUS ON STUDENTS **RADICALIZING** WORKERS.

BERNARDINE DOHRN AND OTHER REGULARS SUCCESSFULLY OFFERED **TWO** PROGRAMS: (1) A **TWO-DAY** NATIONAL ELECTION **STRIKE** AND (2) A PLAN TO RECRUIT **HIGH SCHOOL** STUDENTS.

NEXT THING YOU KNOW WE'LL BE **ROBBING** THE CRADLE.

BUT THE **ELECTION DAY** DEMONSTRATIONS WERE DISAPPOINTING. FAR **FEWER** PEOPLE SHOWED UP THAN WERE **EXPECTED**.

SDS CTION STRIKE AND TRATION

SDS WAS RATTLED BY THIS **DISAPPOINTMENT**, AND CHAPTERS WERE QUICKLY **DIVIDING** INTO HOSTILE **FACTIONS** OVER THE DIRECTION THAT **SDS** SHOULD NOW TAKE. EVEN IN A **MINORITY**, PLERS WERE BETTER **ORGANIZED**.

THEY JUST KEEP COMING **ON** WITH **THEIR** LITTLE RED BOOKS.

RESENTMENT AGAINST THE NATIONAL OFFICE BY **CHAPTER MEMBERS**, ESPECIALLY IN **"MIDDLE AMERICA,"** WAS ALSO **GROWING**.

I DUNNO IF I BUY ALL THIS **MARXIST** STUFF. THAT'S **NOT** WHY I JOINED **SDS**.

To MAKE MATTERS **STILL** WORSE, **GOVERNMENT** ON VARIOUS LEVELS AND UNIVERSITIES HAD **BEGUN** CRACKING DOWN ON **SDS**, INFILTRATING CHAPTERS WITH **AGENTS** FROM THE FBI AND THE LOCAL **"RED SQUADS."** AGENTS OFTEN DID THEIR DIRTY WORK BY **EXAGGERATING** THE **DIFFERENCES** BETWEEN FACTIONS.

DID YOU **HEAR** THAT **ONE** CHAPTER ELECTED A POLICE **AGENT** AS THE **CHAIR**? HE PRETENDED TO BE **MORE** RADICAL THAN **ANYONE** ELSE.

UNDERCOVER POLICE

There was a lot of political **activity**, some **violent**, on college campuses that **fall**, but **SDS** originated **less and less** of it. Students in many places saw **SDS** as only a **part** of the **radical** picture and sometimes the dogmatic, **rhetoric-heavy** part.

WE'RE *LOSING* OUR *VANGUARD* POSITION.

At the **December** national council meeting, **Michael Klonsky's** proposal for a **revolutionary youth movement (RYM)** was accepted by a **vote**. Young people were to be **organized** both **off** and **on** the campus.

HEY, BUDDY, C'LD I TALK TO YOU ABOUT SDS'S REVOLUTIONARY YOUTH MOVEMENT?

REVOLUTIONARY *WHAT?*

As **SDS** continued to **lose** momentum in leading the **radical** students, its leaders **allied** themselves to **African American** groups, **third world** revolutionaries of various other kinds, **labor union** dissidents, and **GI** resistance groups. **Dohrn** especially worked hard to create **alliances.**

SO I *THINK* IT WOULD BE IN *BOTH* OF OUR INTERESTS...

SDS activity in student demonstrations went on, but often **without** good results when conservatives **rallied** with administrators and police. Particularly disturbing was the **defeat** after the long student strike at **San Francisco State.**

S. I. HAYAKAWA: SAN FRANCISCO STATE PRESIDENT AND **STRIKEBREAKER,** FUTURE **REPUBLICAN** POLITICIAN.

THE MORE THE **SDS** NATIONAL OFFICE BECAME **DESPERATE** TO LEAD, THE MORE **RIGID** IDEOLOGICALLY IT **BECAME**. THE STUDENT BASE WAS DRIFTING AWAY.

TRASHING WINDOWS AROUND CAMPUS IS AS *STUPID* AS TALKING ABOUT *CHAIRMAN MAO*.

OGLESBY REMARKED:

ON *EVERY* QUARTER OF THE *WHITE LEFT*, HIGH AND LOW, THE ATTEMPT TO REDUCE THE *NEW LEFT'S* INCHOATE VISION TO THE *OLD LEFT'S* PERFECTED REMEMBRANCE HAS *PRODUCED* A LAYER OF *BEWILDERMENT* AND DEMORALIZATION WHICH NO *COP* WITH HIS CLUB OR *SENATOR* WITH HIS COMMITTEE COULD EVER HAVE INDUCED.

WOMEN BEGAN TO LEAVE *SDS* FOR WOMEN'S GROUPS.

WE'RE ALWAYS LOOKING TO SOMEONE ELSE TO LEAD A *REVOLUTION*. WHY DON'T WE MAKE OUR *OWN*?

GOING INTO ITS **JUNE 1969** CONVENTION, **SDS** WAS IN A **STRANGE** POSITION. ITS **MAJOR** OBSTACLE IN THE GROUP WAS **PROGRESSIVE LABOR**, BUT BY BECOMING **MARXIST-LENINIST, SDS** HAD ACTUALLY BECOME MORE LIKE **PL** IN SOME **KEY** WAYS. THE STRANGEST **PART** WAS THAT **PL** ATTEMPTS TO REACH **REAL** WORKERS HAD PROVED A **FAILURE**. FACTIONS FACED OFF WITH **UNREAL** RHETORIC.

SIR, COULD I...

GET THE HELL **AWAY FROM ME, YOU COMMIE.**

AND THE RHETORIC QUICKLY GOT MORE **UNREAL**. BERNARDINE DOHRN, WHEN **TESTIFYING** BEFORE AN **SDS** PANEL, REMARKED:

I CONSIDER MYSELF A REVOLUTIONARY COMMUNIST.

SDSERS WERE INCREASINGLY **UPSET** THAT ALL THE DEMONSTRATIONS HAD **FAILED** TO STOP OR EVEN SLOW DOWN THE **WAR** IN VIETNAM.

GIVE PEACE A CHANCE

U.S. OUT OF VIET-NAM!

WHAT DID WE ACCOMPLISH WITH ALL THIS?

ND HE AR!

39

THE MAJOR EFFECTS OF THE CAMPUS EFFORTS WERE COMING MORE GRADUALLY AND INTELLECTUALLY, IN BLACK STUDIES, WOMEN'S STUDIES, AND DEMOCRATIC RESTRUCTURING OF SOME UNIVERSITIES.

BLACK STUDIES ON CAMPUS

SDSERS CAME TO THE 1969 CHICAGO SDS CONVENTION FEELING THAT THEY HAD TO MEET THE WORLD'S REVOLUTIONARY RESPONSIBILITIES, INCLUDING THE ABANDONMENT OF NONVIOLENCE.

THAT'S FOR HO CHI MINH!

SDS LEADERS DETERMINED THAT THEY WOULD HAVE TO MAKE SDS TOUGHER AND MORE TIGHTLY STRUCTURED, MORE LIKE THE BLACK PANTHERS AND THIRD WORLD REVOLUTIONARY GROUPS.

41

In order to achieve this kind of membership, **SDS** leaders determined to **eliminate** pockets of resistance, particularly the **Progressive Labor Party** faction.

THEY **WANT** TO GET RID OF US. WE WON'T **LET** THEM!

By this time, members and supporters of PL constituted as much as a **third** of **SDS**, mainly because such a **small** proportion of chapter **activists** actually bothered to **join** the national organization.

I THINK YOU **SHOULD** CONSIDER **JOINING** OUR FACTION.

At first PL proved only an irritant to regular **SDSers** in most places. In **some** places, PLers **proved** themselves doggedly **sincere**, especially trying to organize low-wage, nonunion **workers**. But the differences **between** the factions grew at **every** level. PLers not **only** had short hair, they denounced **marijuana**.

DRUGS ARE A **PLOT** BY THE **RULING** CLASS!

PLers were reluctant even to demonstrate for **civil rights**, because they feared that it would **upset** the still **reactionary workers** whom they hoped to **radicalize**.

WE CAN'T **ALIENATE** THE **WORKERS!**

PL DISAPPROVED IN PARTICULAR OF **EVERY** KIND OF **NATIONALISM**, INCLUDING THE **BLACK** NATIONALISM OF GROUPS LIKE THE **BLACK PANTHERS**. THEY INSISTED THAT **AFRICAN AMERICANS** SHOULD **NOT** BE GIVEN **SPECIAL** TREATMENT IN A REVOLUTIONARY SITUATION.

SORRY, BUT TO US YOU'RE JUST LIKE **ANYONE** ELSE.

THEY ALSO DISAPPROVED OF **SDS** SIDING WITH **COMMUNIST** FIGHTERS IN **VIETNAM**, SINCE PL WAS **PRO-CHINESE** AND **ANTI-RUSSIAN** COMMUNIST, AND THE **RUSSIANS** WERE AIDING THE **VIETNAMESE**.

43

SDS HAD PRINTED A SPECIAL **CONVENTION** EDITION OF ITS **"NEW LEFT NOTES"** IN WHICH IT **JUSTIFIED** ITS POSITIONS, ENTITLED: **"YOU DON'T NEED A WEATHERMAN TO KNOW WHICH WAY THE WIND BLOWS,"** TAKEN FROM A SONG BY **BOB DYLAN**. THEN AN ANTI-**PL DOHRN**–LED SPLINTER GROUP, **"WEATHERMEN,"** EMERGED.

new left notes

Convention Edition

IN THE **"WEATHERMEN"** VISION, THERE WAS LITTLE OR NO PLACE FOR **WHITES** IN THE UPCOMING **REVOLUTION**. ONLY A RELATIVE **HANDFUL** OF WHITES (INCLUDING **THEMSELVES**) COULD BE EFFECTIVE AS **ALLIES** TO THE BLACK AND **THIRD WORLD** REVOLUTIONARIES.

THEY'VE WRITTEN OFF **WHITES, ALL WHITES,** INCLUDING MY **BLUE-COLLAR** RELATIVES. I'M NO **PL**ER, BUT THIS IS **CRAZY.**

THIS CALLS FOR THE **FORMATION** OF A **"REVOLUTIONARY PARTY"** SET IN URBAN AREAS AND ORGANIZED INTO A **CADRE** SYSTEM, EFFECTIVE SECRECY, AND A **"CENTRALIZED ORGANIZATION."**

NEO TROTSKYIST PROGRESSIVE SOCIALIST RADICAL ACTION CLUB FOR INTERNATIONAL PEACE

SOCIALIST PROGRESSIVE CLUB FOR INTERNAT'L DEMOCRACY THRU RADICAL PROTOTROTSKYIST ACTION

APOLOGIES TO RADICAL AMERICA KOMIKS

THE **OLD SDS**, THE **LOOSE** NATIONAL ORGANIZATION WITH FREEWHEELING DEBATE, IS **DEAD**, DONE AWAY BY THE **WEATHERMEN** AS MUCH AS **PL**. THEY REALLY ARE LIKE **PL** THAT **WAY**, BUT THEY **DON'T** REALIZE IT.

THE PL VIEW WAS NOT APPEALING TO MOST OF THE YOUNGSTERS ON HAND. BUT THE **WEATHERMEN** POSITION ALSO **ALIENATED** MANY VETERAN **SDS** MEMBERS. SOME WALKED OUT, **DISGUSTED**.

THEY WANT TO **STOP** WORKING WITH **COLLEGE STUDENTS.** THEY ARE RUNNING **AWAY** FROM THEIR **MEMBERSHIP!**

ABBIE HOFFMAN DIDN'T CLAIM TO GRASP THE ENORMITY OF WHAT WAS HAPPENING — OR HE SAW HOW **CRAZY** IT HAD **BECOME**.

THROUGHOUT THE CONFERENCE I MARVELED AT HOW **LITTLE I UNDERSTOOD** WHAT WAS BEING **SAID.**

THE **SECOND** DAY WAS DEVOTED TO **ACRIMONIOUS** DEBATE BETWEEN THE WEATHERMEN AND PL:

YOU GUYS DON'T HAVE A LEG TO STAND ON.

I COULD SAY THE SAME ABOUT YOU.

THAT EVENING SOME **LEADERS** FROM THE **PUERTO RICAN YOUNG LORDS,** THE **CHICANO BROWN BERETS,** AND THE **BLACK PANTHERS** ATTENDED THE CONVENTION, ALL OF WHOM THE **WEATHERMEN** THOUGHT WERE **ALLIES.**

BUT THE BLACK PANTHER PARTY MEMBERS DEEPLY EMBARRASSED THE WEATHERMEN WITH THEIR SEXIST REMARKS.

WITH REGARD TO WOMEN'S LIBERATION, WE BELIEVE IN PUSSY POWER!

ANOTHER BLACK PANTHER SPEAKER RESPONDED TO THE CROWD BY TAUNTING THEM:

LET ME EXPLAIN, WOMEN DO HAVE A PART, A STRATEGIC POSITION IN THE REVOLUTION – PRONE.

ENRAGED FEMINISTS STARTED TO SHOUT:

FIGHT MALE CHAUVINISTS!!

THE BLACK PANTHER, LOOKING FOR SUPPORT, BERATED PL.

YOU ARMCHAIR MARXISTS! WE'RE OUT THERE DOING THE FIGHTING AND SHEDDING BLOOD, AND YOU HAVEN'T GOTTEN A SCRATCH.

THE NEXT EVENING THE CONVENTION RECEIVED A MESSAGE FROM THE BLACK PANTHERS.

"AFTER LONG STUDY AND INVESTIGATION OF STUDENTS FOR A DEMOCRATIC SOCIETY, AND THE PROGRESSIVE LABOR PARTY IN PARTICULAR, WE HAVE COME TO THE CONCLUSION THAT THE PROGRESSIVE LABOR PARTY HAS DEVIATED FROM MARXIST-LENINIST IDEOLOGY ON THE NATIONAL QUESTION AND THE RIGHT OF SELF-DETERMINATION OF ALL OPPRESSED PEOPLE..."

"...IF THE PROGRESSIVE LABOR PARTY CONTINUES ITS EGOCENTRIC POLICIES AND REVISIONIST BEHAVIOR, THEY WILL BE CONSIDERED AS COUNTERREVOLUTIONARY TRAITORS AND WILL BE DEALT WITH AS SUCH."

THE CONVENTION WENT INTO BEDLAM, WITH CHARGES AND COUNTERCHARGES EXCHANGED BY PLERS AND THE WEATHERMEN.

BERNARDINE DOHRN GRABBED THE MICROPHONE.

CAN WE STAY IN THE SAME ORGANIZATION WITH PEOPLE WHO DENY THE OPPRESSED?

Through HOURS of arguments THAT evening and the NEXT morning, SDS officials debated what to do with PL.

LET'S DEBATE THEM SOME MORE...

LET'S GO BACK AND JOIN WITH THEM AND GET THROUGH THE WEEKEND...

NO, THEY HAVE TO GO NOW.

FINALLY, ON SATURDAY NIGHT, IMMEDIATE EXPULSION WAS AGREED UPON. DOHRN GOT THE MICROPONE, MADE A HEATED SPEECH, AND EXPELLED PL. THE CONVENTION VOTED TO SUPPORT HER.

PL IS RACIST, ANTICOMMUNIST, AND REACTIONARY!

A HUGE THRONG OF SDSERS WALKED OUT OF THE HALL. SOME LOOKED TRIUMPHANT, OTHERS LOOKED DOWNHEARTED.

49

NATURALLY BOTH THE **WEATHERMEN** AND THEIR SUPPORTERS AND **PL** CLAIMED THEY WERE NOW **IN CHARGE OF SDS. PL** CHOSE AND ELECTED AN **UNOPPOSED** SLATE OF **NEW** OFFICERS.

I NOMINATE **JOHN PENNINGTON** FOR **NATIONAL SECRETARY.**

THE SDS REGULARS MEANWHILE MET IN A CHURCH AND **DECIDED** TO COSPONSOR A MEETING WITH THE **BLACK PANTHERS** AND TO HOLD A "**MASS**" ACTION AGAINST THE VIETNAM WAR.

WE GOTTA **HUMBLE** THE **PIGS!**

IN THE NEXT WEEKS, **PL-SDS** MOVED TO ITS ORGANIZATIONAL HOME BASE IN **BOSTON,** CONFIDENT OF THE **FUTURE.**

WE'VE JUST **TAKEN OVER** THE MOST **IMPORTANT** ORGANIZATION IN **AMERICA.**

BUT **PL** AND ITS **SDS** FACTION HAD NO REAL **APPEAL** TO YOUNG PEOPLE. THEY **NEVER** MADE AN ATTEMPT TO **REACH** THE DEEPLY ALIENATED, DRUG-USING YOUNG WORKERS, BLACK, WHITE, AND **LATINO,** JUST BACK FROM **VIETNAM.** THEIR RANKS THINNED QUICKLY.

WHAT **HAPPENED** TO OUR **FACTION?**

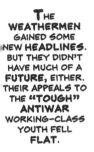

THE WEATHERMEN GAINED SOME NEW HEADLINES. BUT THEY DIDN'T HAVE MUCH OF A FUTURE, EITHER. THEIR APPEALS TO THE "TOUGH" ANTIWAR WORKING-CLASS YOUTH FELL FLAT.

CHECK THIS OUT!

BIG DEAL!

IN OCTOBER 1969 THE WEATHERMEN DIRECTED THEIR "DAYS OF RAGE" IN CHICAGO, RAMPAGING DOWN CITY STREETS, BREAKING STORE AND CAR WINDOWS. BUT THEY TOOK A BEATING FROM THE COPS AND HAD TO GO FURTHER UNDERGROUND.

KLUNK!

WE HAVE GONE UNDERGROUND!

THE WEATHERMEN DECIDED AGAINST MASS ACTION AFTER THAT AND FORMED SMALL CADRES DEDICATED TO THE TASK OF REVOLUTIONARY VIOLENCE. THEY IMAGINED THEMSELVES LIKE THE VIETCONG OR NATIONAL LIBERATION MOVEMENT OF VIETNAM.

51

LOCAL
SCENES

This section of *Students for a Democratic Society: A Graphic History* goes in a different direction. SDSers' own lives tell us something that an overview of their collective political experience alone cannot reveal. It is also something best seen by looking in the rearview mirror of history.

The "SDS Years" seemed to go by terribly fast for participants not yet in their thirties. And then, altogether unexpectedly, time for many former activists slowed down to a veritable crawl. Thousands found political opportunities here and there, campaigning for the election of progressive local officials, taking part in new interracial coalitions, working against nuclear power, and so on. Still, the normalizing day-to-day continuity of careers and family took over, leaving many of those seen in this book's previous pages badly distraught, others relieved of the burden of transforming society, and most feeling a mixture of strongly contradictory emotions.

Later on, in middle age, something about those youthful days reversed the process by making the exciting times monumental and enduring in memory. Each day in the heart of a great mobilization now looked a week or a month long. Nothing remotely like it was to happen again in their lives. And thus an unavoidable insight sank in: the great events had always been deeply personal as well as political, and local at least as much as national or international.

The second section of this volume is no less and no more "real" than the first section. The history of SDS is—far more than, say, that of the Democratic or Republican Party—really the history of its members, sometimes intimately connected with developments in the national movement, sometimes so local and so personal that the connections could better be described as metaphorical. So little institutional money, power, career prospect, or any other perquisite was at stake, so suspicious did many chapter activists remain toward the National Office, that it could hardly be otherwise.

The choice of themes in the following pages is deliberate even if, inevitably, they are also incomplete. The community-organizing impulse, the campus, the war, the draft, the counterculture of music and art, connections and conflicts between men and women, are present in practically every presentation of 1960's Movement history. The choice of particulars, of places and people, is more arbitrary. A notice on the Internet during 2005–06 actually urged former SDSers to send stories and pictures. A generous handful did. Those self-chosen are, at least, faithfully representative of many others unarticulated here. Future comic art histories of the sixties are certain to have more to say.

The stories range, in any case, from New York to California and many spots in between. Most often they are in one sense or another "from the heartland," perfectly ordinary SDSers behaving in ways perfectly ordinary for SDSers. One of the larger conceits of American life at large is that key developments most often take place in New York City or Washington, D.C., with California added to the list in recent decades. But the SDS activities presented here, and the personalities too, could just as well have been described in Boulder; in Norman, Oklahoma; or in Eugene, Oregon, among other places, and the content might not be different—except, of course, for the vital personal details of those involved in them. Succeed or fail, SDSers everywhere lived a crucial moment in national history to its fullest.

WHITE BOY NARRATIVE

FROM CROWN HEIGHTS TO MORNINGSIDE HEIGHTS

STORY BY MARK NAISON

ART BY GARY DUMM

THIS IS A LOVE STORY... OR TWO LOVE STORIES...THE SMALL STORY HAPPY, THE BIG STORY NOT SO HAPPY. BUT BOTH PART OF THE STRUGGLE.

C'MON NOW, DINNER'S READY!

I GREW UP IN A REDBRICK **APARTMENT** BUILDING AT THE INTERSECTION OF **LEFFERTS** AND **KINGSTON** AVENUES IN THE **CROWN HEIGHTS** SECTION OF **BROOKLYN.**

MOST OF THE **JEWS, INCLUDING** MY FAMILY, LIVED IN THE **SIX-STORY ELEVATOR BUILDINGS.**

KAY BROS. FLORIST

IN THE **1950'S** IT WAS A PEACEFUL NEIGHBORHOOD POPULATED LARGELY BY **SECOND-** AND **THIRD-** GENERATION **JEWS** AND **ITALIANS.** PARENTS WORKED HARD TO HIDE THE SCARS INFLICTED BY THE **DEPRES-SION,** THE **HOLOCAUST,** AND THE TERRORS OF THE **JIM CROW** SOUTH...TO GIVE THEIR CHILDREN A FEEL-ING THAT THE WORLD WAS FUNDAMENTALLY **BENIGN,** A PLACE OF ADVENTURE AND OPPORTUNITY WHERE **NO** ACCOMPLISHMENTS WERE OUT OF REACH.

NEIGHBORHOOD LIFE WAS **RITUALIZED**, GIVING **CROWN HEIGHTS** A VILLAGE–LIKE **ATMOSPHERE**.

ON WEEKDAYS MEN WENT OFF TO WORK, WHILE **WOMEN** WALKED THEIR CHILDREN TO SCHOOL, **CONVERSED** WITH ONE ANOTHER FROM APARTMENT WINDOWS, AND **DRIED** THEIR LAUNDRY ON **CLOTHESLINES** THAT HUNG FROM OR BETWEEN **BUILDINGS** OR STOOD IN BACKYARDS.

THERE WERE **STILL** STREET **PEDDLERS**, A ROVING **KNIFE** SHARPENER, A **RAG** PICKER IN A HORSE–DRAWN **WAGON**.

ANY OLD CLOTHES?!

NO ONE HAD MORE THAN **TWO** BEDROOMS, BUT THAT SEEMED **LUXURIOUS** TO RESIDENTS. CARS AND TELEVISION SETS HAD BECOME **IMPORTANT** FEATURES OF FAMILY LIFE.

YOO–HOO, MOLLY GOLDBERG!

FAMILIES GATHERED TO WATCH FAVORITE **SHOWS** AND PLANNED WEEKEND **TRIPS** TO THEIR RELATIVES.

THE VITALITY OF STREET LIFE REMAINED THE NEIGHBORHOOD'S **DEFINING** CHAR–ACTERISTIC. **KIDS** USED **EVERY** AVAILABLE **SPACE** FOR GAMES AND CONTESTS.

GIRLS WERE **PROHIBITED** FROM ACTIVITIES THAT INVOLVED PHYSICAL **AGGRESSIVENESS** OR THE **RISK** OF GETTING DIRTY.

THERE WEREN'T MANY **BLACK** FAMILIES...AND THE JEWS THAT I GREW UP WITH WERE POLITICALLY **LIBERAL** OR LEFT-WING, UNWILLING TO EXPRESS RACIAL **HOSTILITY** IN FRONT OF THEIR CHILDREN. I **NEVER** HEARD A NEIGHBOR OR MEMBER OF MY FAMILY USE THE WORD **"NIGGER."** PARENTS REVERTED TO YIDDISH WHEN TALKING ABOUT **BLACK** PEOPLE. ADULTS SEEMED **ASHAMED** TO TALK ABOUT **RACIAL** ISSUES.

...DIE SCHWARTZE...

BUT **ALMOST** EVERY **JEWISH** FAMILY IN OUR NEIGHBORHOOD HAD **BLACK** WOMEN COME TO **CLEAN** THEIR APARTMENTS OR HELP CARE FOR THEIR CHILDREN. **JEWISH** WOMEN REFERRED TO THESE WORKERS AS THEIR **"GIRLS,"** ALTHOUGH THE WOMEN WERE OFTEN **OLDER** THAN THEY WERE. **EVERY** MORNING THEY ARRIVED IN A **GROUP** ON THE **BUS,** AND LEFT BY THE **SAME** ROUTE.

MY MOTHER EMPLOYED A **BLACK** WOMAN NAMED **ADLER** AND **INSISTED** THAT I TREAT HER WITH **RESPECT.** BUT WHY WAS SOMEONE SO **CAPABLE** AND INTELLIGENT **CLEANING** OUR HOUSE? WHY **WASN'T** SHE A TEACHER, LIKE MY **MOTHER?**

I GREW UP **"TOO SMART."** MY PARENTS PLACED ME A GRADE AHEAD, WHICH I **HATED.** I MADE UP FOR IT BY BEING ATHLETIC AND **TOUGH.** MY FATHER **DRAGGED** ME OFF THE FOOTBALL FIELD. I RESPONDED BY BEING **REBELLIOUS.** THEY WITHHELD **TELEVISION** PRIVILEGES, **WASHED** MY MOUTH OUT WITH **SOAP,** AND **SLAPPED** MY FACE.

57

MY CLOSEST ALLY WAS MY UNCLE MAC. HIS SONS WERE THE BEST YOUNG ATHLETES IN THE NEIGHBORHOOD, AND WE ALL WATCHED GAMES TOGETHER ON HIS TELEVISION SET. BLACK ATHLETES WERE JUST COMING INTO PROMINENCE. WE HAD BLACK SPORTS HEROES WITHOUT EVER REMARKING ON THEIR COLOR.

...HE GOES TO THE HOOP AND SCORES!

IT WAS THE SAME THING IN MUSIC: WE LOVED ROCK 'N' ROLL. IT BROUGHT US TOGETHER WITH GIRLS, WHO UP UNTIL THEN HAD SEEMED LIKE A SEPARATE SPECIES.

I STUDIED SPORTS FIGURES AND ROCK 'N' ROLL STARS WITH THE SAME PASSION THAT MY PARENTS HAD APPROACHED SCIENCE AND HISTORY.

RACIAL ATTITUDES WERE CHANGING IN THE NEIGHBORHOOD. JEWS BEGAN TO TALK ABOUT MOVING TO ALL-WHITE AREAS, WHILE I IDENTIFIED WITH MY BLACK FRIENDS. WHEN I JOINED THE ANTIDISCRIMINATION CAMPAIGN LED BY CORE IN MY NEIGHBORHOOD, MY PARENTS TOLD ME:

JEWS ALWAYS GET IN TROUBLE WHEN THEY TRY TO HELP OTHER PEOPLE.

AND THEN I WAS ADMITTED TO **COLUMBIA**. IT WAS A DIFFERENT WORLD. **SPORTS** WAS ONE OF THE FEW DOMAINS IN WHICH STUDENTS FROM **WORKING-CLASS** BACKGROUNDS AND **PUBLIC** SCHOOLS **SET** THE TONE. BUT THE **JOCK** CULTURE WAS **DEEPLY** RACIST AND BLACK STUDENTS WERE FEW.

BUT BY MY **SOPHOMORE** YEAR, I GOT RID OF MY **CREW CUT**, GREW A **GOATEE**, AND **STARTED** FREQUENTING **COFFEE** SHOPS AND **JAZZ** CLUBS.

I WENT TO MY **FIRST** MEETING OF THE COLUMBIA **CORE** CHAPTER AND **VOLUNTEERED** TO DO TUTORING AND TENANT ORGANIZING IN **EAST HARLEM**.

CORE WAS A **NEW** MOVEMENT. WHEN I WENT TO A MEETING, THE OTHER PARTICIPANTS HAD A **BOHEMIAN** APPEARANCE...**WOMEN** WITH HAIR DOWN TO THEIR SHOULDERS WORE LONG, FLOWING **DRESSES**...MEN HAD BEARDS AND MUSTACHES, COWBOY BOOTS, AND JEANS. WE WERE **DOING** SOMETHING...AND WE WERE THE **HIPPEST** PEOPLE ON THE CAMPUS.

59

I DECIDED TO **WORK** IN **HARLEM**.

MOST OF THE APARTMENTS I ENTERED SEEMED LIKE **OASES** OF ORDER AND PRIDE IN THE MIDST OF **CHAOS**. THE VALUES AND GOALS SEEMED STRIKINGLY **FAMILIAR**...

...JUST LIKE THOSE OF THE **UPWARDLY MOBILE** FAMILIES I'D GROWN UP WITH...

...BUT THE **PROBLEMS** THEY DESCRIBED TO ME WERE **OUTSIDE** MY EXPERIENCE. HERE WERE **ADMIRABLE** PEOPLE TRAPPED IN **INTOLERABLE** CONDITIONS: WATER DAMAGE FROM A **LEAKING** ROOF...

...INTERMITTENT **HEAT**, BROKEN FRONT DOORS, AND HUGE **RATS** TERRORIZING THEIR CHILDREN. I WAS DETERMINED TO **HELP** THEM.

TWO **NIGHTS** A WEEK I WOULD **LEAVE** CAMPUS, SPEAK TO FAMILIES ABOUT THEIR **TROUBLES**, HELP THEM FILL OUT OFFICIAL CITY **FORMS**, AND ENCOURAGE THE FORMATION OF AN ORGANIZED **COUNCIL** TO NEGOTIATE WITH THE **LANDLORD**.

I STARTED TO FEEL AT **HOME** ON THE STREETS OF **EAST HARLEM**, TO ENJOY THE SMELL OF **LATIN** COOKING, THE POUNDING RHYTHMS OF LATIN **MUSIC**, AND, ABOVE ALL, THE EXHILARATING **FEELING** OF **DEFYING** FEAR AND PREJUDICE. BUT **COLUMBIA UNIVERSITY** WAS PUSHING THESE PEOPLE OUT, **DEMOLISHING** THEIR BUILDINGS TO ERECT **NEW** ONES.

WE MADE **PROGRESS**. WE GOT MEDIA ATTENTION. I SHOWED UP AT THE LANDLORD'S OFFICE IN MY **BEST** SUIT. ONE LANDLADY SHOWED ME HER **TATTOO**: SHE HAD BEEN IN THE **NAZI** DEATH CAMPS, AND SHE DID **NOT** WANT TO HEAR ABOUT ANY **NON-JEW** BEING **VICTIMIZED**. BUT SOME **DID** IMPROVE THEIR BUILDINGS.

IN THE **SPRING** OF MY SOPHOMORE YEAR MY HITCHHIKING **PARTNER** FROM **SUMMER** CAMP, ANDY GOODMAN, WAS **MURDERED** IN MISSISSIPPI AS HE TRIED TO **REGISTER** BLACK CITIZENS TO **VOTE** IN THE **MISSISSIPPI** FREEDOM **SUMMER**.

CHANEY

SCHWERNER

GOODMAN

ANDY HAD BEEN **KIDNAPPED** AND **KILLED** ALONG WITH A BLACK **MISSISSIPPI** RESIDENT, **JAMES CHANEY**, AND A VETERAN **SNCC** ACTIVIST, **MICHAEL SCHWERNER**, BY MEMBERS OF THE **KU KLUX KLAN**.

I WAS GROWING MORE **RADICAL** AS THE CAMPUS **DIVIDED** BETWEEN STUDENT PROTESTERS — MOSTLY JEWISH **MEN** AND **WOMEN** WORKING TOGETHER AND LIVING A **BOHEMIAN** LIFESTYLE – AND THE **ATHLETES**, WHO WERE ALL **MALE**, MAINLY **CATHOLIC**.

UNION NOW

UNION

THE **UNION** DRIVE BY **UNIVERSITY CAFETERIA** WORKERS DIVIDED THINGS EVEN **FURTHER**. IN RESPONSE I STARTED MARCHING ON PICKET LINES IN MY **VARSITY** "C" JACKET. BUT TO MY TEAMMATES, THE **IDEA** OF THE **BEATNIK** PROTESTER AS ROMANTIC **HERO**, **MORE** ATTRACTIVE TO WOMEN THAN THE HYPERMASCULINE WHITE ATHLETE, EVOKED ONLY **RAGE** AND **ENVY**.

THEN IT HAPPENED: I MET THE BLACK WOMAN I WOULD **LIVE** WITH FOR THE NEXT **SIX YEARS. NOT** AT A **POLITICAL** EVENT, BUT AT A **PARTY**...HELD BY THE ONLY **TRULY** INTERRACIAL GROUP ON CAMPUS, **"THE FRIENDS OF THE COLUMBIA BASKETBALL TEAM."**

WE **DANCED** AND ENDED UP GOING **BACK** TO HER APARTMENT...WHERE I **COULDN'T** PERFORM. BUT THE EXCITEMENT OF THE OCCASION AND HER **KINDNESS** MADE ME LOOK AT HER **CLOSELY:** SHE WAS THE **MOS** BEAUTIFUL WOMAN I HAD EVER BEEN WITH. WALKING **BACK** TO CAMPUS, I **REALIZED** THAT AN **IMPORTAN** PIECE OF MY **LIFE** HAD JUST FALLEN INTO **PLACE.**

RUTHIE'S SISTERS LIVED IN THE **BRONX,** AND NO ONE EXPRESSED A **SECOND** THOUGHT ABOUT AN INTERRACIAL COUPLE GOING THERE TOGETHER. BUT THE MORE TIME WE SPENT **TOGETHER,** THE MORE **HOSTILITY** WE RECEIVED, ESPECIALLY FROM OLDER **JEWISH** WOMEN AND DOWN-AND-OUT **BLACK** MEN...WHITE WORKING-CLASS **TEENAGERS** WERE ACTUALLY THE **MOST** INTOLERANT.

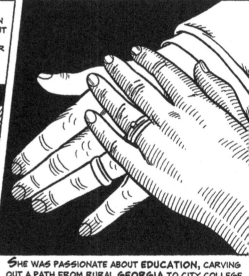

SHE WAS PASSIONATE ABOUT **EDUCATION,** CARVING OUT A PATH FROM RURAL **GEORGIA** TO CITY COLLEGE AND **PROFESSIONAL** STATUS. I WANTED TO BECOME THE **SCHOLAR** WHO WOULD EXPLORE **AMERICA'S** RACE PROBLEM. PROUD OF BEING **PIONEERS** IN CHALLENGING RACIAL **BARRIERS,** WE WERE **HAPPY** WITH SO MANY **FRIENDS** WHO SUPPORTED AND NURTURED US.

IN EARLY 1966 I TOOK THE SUBWAY TO ALL-WHITE REGO PARK, WHERE MY PARENTS HAD MOVED. MY FATHER WAS DYING OF CANCER, AND MY MOTHER, A SCHOOLTEACHER, WAS ANGRY AT DISOBEDIENT BLACK AND PUERTO RICAN STUDENTS. I HAD MADE UP MY MIND TO TELL THEM ABOUT HER.

AFTER I TOLD MY FATHER FIRST, HE SAID QUIETLY, "YOUR MOTHER WILL NEVER ACCEPT THIS."

MY MOTHER, THE TOUGHEST PERSON THAT I EVER KNEW, RESPONDED BY THREATENING TO COMMIT SUICIDE.

DO YOU WANT ME TO KILL MYSELF?

THEY ACCEPTED ME IN THEIR APARTMENT ON THE CONDITION THAT I'D NEVER BRING RUTHIE OVER AND NEVER MENTION HER AGAIN!

GO BACK TO RUSSIA!

JOCKS FOR PEACE

JEWS AND NIGGERS, GO BACK TO RUSSIA!

BY 1967, BACK ON CAMPUS, I HAD JOINED SDS AND THE ANTIWAR MOVEMENT. SDS MEMBERS SEEMED SO OVERLY INTELLECTUAL, BUT THEY WERE ALSO TIRELESS AND COURAGEOUS. WHEN THEY HELD MARCHES ON CAMPUS, I MARCHED IN AN INTERRACIAL CONTINGENT OF THIRTY ATHLETES WHO CARRIED SIGNS READING "JOCKS FOR PEACE." WHEN FOOTBALL PLAYERS AND WRESTLERS SURROUNDED US, THEIR FACES RED WITH ANGER AND VEINS BULGING FROM THEIR NECKS, CHALLENGING US TO FIGHT, I WAS SHOCKED. I'D NEVER SEEN SUCH ANGER ON CAMPUS. ON A SINGLE AFTERNOON WE GOT A GLIMPSE OF HOW DIVISIVE VIETNAM WOULD BE.

RUTHIE AND I WERE MORE ATTRACTED TO THE HIPPIE/ANTIWAR CULTURE THAN TO THE POLITICOS... BUT THERE WAS NO ESCAPE. TWO WEEKS AFTER MARTIN LUTHER KING, JR.'S DEATH, COLUMBIA SDS AND THE STUDENT AFRICAN AMERICAN SOCIETY (SAS) JOINTLY CALLED A RALLY AT THE SUNDIAL ON THE CENTER OF CAMPUS TO DEMAND THAT COLUMBIA STOP THE CONSTRUCTION OF THE GYM PLANNED IN MORNINGSIDE PARK, WITHDRAW THE SUSPENSION OF ANTIWAR PROTESTERS, AND SEVER TIES TO THE OMINOUS INSTITUTE OF DEFENSE ANALYSIS CLOSE TO CAMPUS.

FIVE HUNDRED STUDENTS SHOWED UP...THE LARGEST NUMBER I HAD EVER SEEN TOGETHER ON CAMPUS.

AFTER WE MARCHED TO THE PRESIDENT'S OFFICE AND TO THE GYM SITE, SOMEBODY YELLED:

LET'S TAKE A BUILDING!

HAMILTON HALL WAS COMPLETELY UNGUARDED. IT WAS NOT THE ORIGINAL OBJECT OF THE PROTEST, BUT OCCUPYING IT GAVE US LEVERAGE THAT NO STUDENT PROTESTERS EVER HAD THERE.

THE WEDDING
WITHIN THE OCCUPATION

WELL, **FIRST** THERE WERE THE DEMANDS...THERE WAS NO **COMPROMISE** POSSIBLE ON THE **AMNESTY** DEMANDS. WE WOULD **NOT** LET EACH OTHER BE **PUNISHED** FOR WHAT WE ALL DID TO STOP THE **WAR MACHINE**. AND WHAT THEY HATED **MOST** WAS THAT WE FOUND ALL THAT EVIDENCE IN **GRAYSON KIRK'S** OFFICE. THEY HATED THAT! WE KNEW **WHERE** THE BODIES WERE BURIED... LITERALLY!

WE WERE IN **FAYERWEATHER HALL**...IT WAS MORE **SHAKY**, IT WASN'T SOLID LIKE **MATH** AND **LOW**, WHERE IT WAS HARD TO GET IN. YOU COULD **ALWAYS** GET INTO **FAYERWEATHER**, THERE WERE ALWAYS **NEW** PEOPLE, AND THEY NEEDED TO BE **CONVERTED**, BASICALLY, INTO WHAT WE BELIEVED. ESPECIALLY SOMETIMES WHEN CERTAIN **LIBERAL** PROFESSORS WOULD COME AROUND AND SAY:

YOU'VE **WON!**

TIME TO LEAVE...

BUT THEY WANTED A **COMPROMISE** THAT **DIDN'T** INVOLVE **AMNESTY**. THE ADMINISTRATION WANTED REVENGE AND WOULDN'T PROMISE. NOT UNTIL WE **WON.**

WHAT DID YOU **THINK** ABOUT THE **LEADERS**, THE **SDSERS?**

YOU HAD TO GIVE THEM **CREDIT** FOR BEING **GUTSY**. THEY WERE ALSO VERY BIG ON LETTING EVERYONE SPEAK. **BLACK** KIDS CAME IN FROM THE NEIGHBORHOOD AND **SAID** WHAT THEY WANTED. FREELANCE **RADICALS** FROM AROUND THE CITY CAME IN; SOME OF THEM HAD A LOT TO SAY AND SOME JUST **SHOT** OFF THEIR MOUTHS. SOME OF THE CAMPUS **SDS** LEADERS ALSO SEEMED – **HOW** CAN I **PUT** IT – SORT OF **DUMB**, OR **SO** PREOCCUPIED WITH BEING THEMSELVES.

IT WAS ALMOST AS **IMPORTANT** FOR THEM TO SIT AT THE **PRESIDENT'S** DESK AND SMOKE HIS **CIGARS** AS IT WAS TO FIND THE DOCUMENTS.

THEY ALSO DIDN'T SEEM TO **NOTICE** THE PRACTICAL THINGS. WELL, THE **TWO** OF US WERE OLDER, **23-24**, AND **MOST** OF THE STUDENTS WERE **21** OR YOUNGER. WE WERE **NATURALLY** MORE **MATURE**.

SO MUCH ABOUT THE OCCUPATION WAS **PRACTICAL.** WE WERE IN A GUERRILLA-LIKE SITUATION **PART** OF THE TIME...WE **NEEDED** TO HAVE A WET CLOTH FOR EVERYONE WHEN WE WOULD GET TEAR-GASSED. WE NEEDED TO TAKE **CARE** OF A **LOT** OF BUSINESSES, LIKE GETTING PEOPLE FED, MAKING SURE PEOPLE COULD STAY **CLEAN** – ALL OF **THAT** IN **ADDITION** TO **POLITICS.**

DIDN'T YOU **TWO** ACTUALLY GET **MARRIED** DURING THE **OCCUPATION?**

OH, **YES!** WE WERE ALREADY LIVING **TOGETHER** AND **PLANNING** TO GET MARRIED. IT WASN'T A **DECISION** MADE ON THE SPOT. BUT ON THIS **SUNDAY** NIGHT, THINGS WERE VERY **TENSE.** WE THOUGHT THAT **FAYERWEATHER** MIGHT **CAPITULATE** AND LEAVE THE **OTHER** BUILDINGS TO **FIGHT** IT OUT.

THE **PAGEANT PLAYERS** CAME AND DID A **PLAY** ABOUT THE KING AND QUEEN BEING **OVERTHROWN** BY THE PEOPLE. AND THERE WAS A **LOT** OF DRUMMING, PROBABLY BECAUSE THERE WERE A LOT OF **HIPPIES** IN FAYERWEATHER, TOO. THEY BROUGHT IN DRUMS.

THEN, AS **THIS** WAS GOING ON, A FRIEND OF OURS SAID, "THERE'S A **MOVE** TO GET YOU **TWO** MARRIED." AND WE SAID, "**SURE,** WHY THE **HELL** NOT!" THE CAMPUS CHAPLIN, BILL STARR, CLIMBED IN ONE OF THE WINDOWS. MEANWHILE, SOMEBODY WENT OUT AND **GOT** ME A PAIR OF **WHITE** JEANS AND A **WHITE** SWEATER MY SIZE. AND I GOT LOADED UP WITH **ALL** THE JEWELRY THAT **ANYBODY** HAD IN THE PLACE.

IT WAS A **BLACK POWER** PIN, WITH A BUNCH OF **LOVE** BEADS.

RIGHT...SOMEBODY, SOME WOMAN WHOSE **NAME** I **NEVER** FOUND OUT, HANDED ME A RING AND SAID, "HERE, THIS WAS MY **GRANDMOTHER'S.** I WANT **YOU** TO HAVE IT." SO **RICHARD** AND I AND **BILL** WENT OUT ON A BALCONY...AND HE PRONOUNCED US **CHILDREN** OF THE **NEW AGE.**

SOMEHOW, SOMEBODY HAD **GOTTEN THREE HUNDRED** CANDLES...AND IT WAS ALL BEING **PHOTOGRAPHED** BY **NEWSREEL.** THERE WERE AT **LEAST THREE HUNDRED** PEOPLE CARRYING CANDLES...IT WAS A PHENOMENALLY **MOVING** SIGHT.

AND WE HAD A **WEDDING CAKE!** AND PEOPLE WERE SAYING, "IT'S **JUST LIKE** AT 'THE BATTLE OF ALGIERS,'" BECAUSE IN THAT **MOVIE** THERE'S A **WONDERFUL** SCENE WHERE PEOPLE ARE **MARRIED** UNDER **REVOLUTIONARY** AUTHORITY.

BATTLE OF ALGIERS

IT WAS AN **ECSTATIC MOMENT!**

WE ALL WENT OUT AND **MARCHED** AROUND CAMPUS WITH PEOPLE **BANGING** ON POTS AND PANS, EVERYBODY TAKING **PICTURES,** THE TV CAMERAS WERE THERE...IT WAS SHEER **MADNESS.** IF YOU REMEMBER THE **NEWSREEL** FILM, IT CUT ALMOST IMMEDIATELY FROM **THERE** TO THE BUST. THE BUST WAS **24** HOURS IN THE FUTURE, BUT THAT'S HOW WE **FELT.**

THAT WAS THE **NEXT** THING TO **HAPPEN.** BUT, OF COURSE, WE HAD A **HONEYMOON.** SOMEBODY HAD **KEYS** TO A FACULTY **OFFICE:** WE HAD A HONEYMOON **SUITE** OF OUR OWN.

⑬

YES, WITH A **RUG** ON THE FLOOR. THE NEXT DAY IT WAS ON THE **COVER** OF THE **"DAILY NEWS."** WE REALIZED THAT WE HAD TO **LET** OUR PARENTS **KNOW.** SO WE **CALLED** THEM, AND THEY TOOK IT **WELL.** THEY WERE GLAD WE WERE IN THE BUILDINGS...I MEAN, **MY** PARENTS. THEY WERE **RELIEVED** THAT WE GOT **MARRIED,** NO MATTER **WHAT** THE CIRCUMSTANCES.

YOUR PARENTS **WEREN'T** SO HAPPY?

NO. IT WAS THEIR **USUAL REFRAIN...**

WHEN IS HE GOING TO **GROW UP?**

WHEN THE **STORY** APPEARED IN THE **"PHILADELPHIA DAILY NEWS"** MY **MOTHER** SAW THE PICTURES. LATER ON SHE CALLED ME UP AND SAID, "YOU KNOW, YOU COULD HAVE GONE **HOME** AND PUT ON A **DRESS."** BUT THEY WERE **HAPPY** AND MADE A SUBSTANTIAL **CONTRIBUTION** TO OUR **BAIL MONEY** THE **NEXT** DAY.

HOW DID IT **FEEL** TO GET **MARRIED** LIKE **THAT?**

IT WAS **WONDERFUL!** THERE WAS **NOTHING** LIKE IT...IT INVOLVED SO MANY PEOPLE, A **COMMON** PURPOSE, AND EVERYONE WAS REALLY **ECSTATIC** OVER IT.

END OF INTERLUDE

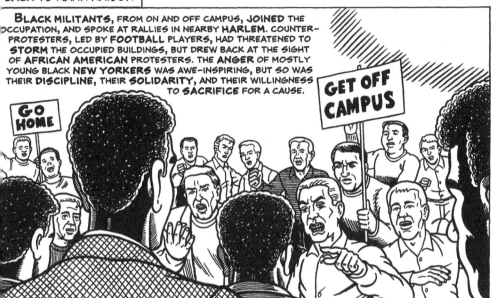

BLACK MILITANTS, FROM ON AND OFF CAMPUS, JOINED THE OCCUPATION, AND SPOKE AT RALLIES IN NEARBY HARLEM. COUNTER-PROTESTERS, LED BY FOOTBALL PLAYERS, HAD THREATENED TO STORM THE OCCUPIED BUILDINGS, BUT DREW BACK AT THE SIGHT OF AFRICAN AMERICAN PROTESTERS. THE ANGER OF MOSTLY YOUNG BLACK NEW YORKERS WAS AWE-INSPIRING, BUT SO WAS THEIR DISCIPLINE, THEIR SOLIDARITY, AND THEIR WILLINGNESS TO SACRIFICE FOR A CAUSE.

GO HOME

GET OFF CAMPUS

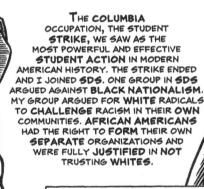

THE COLUMBIA OCCUPATION, THE STUDENT STRIKE, WE SAW AS THE MOST POWERFUL AND EFFECTIVE STUDENT ACTION IN MODERN AMERICAN HISTORY. THE STRIKE ENDED AND I JOINED SDS. ONE GROUP IN SDS ARGUED AGAINST BLACK NATIONALISM. MY GROUP ARGUED FOR WHITE RADICALS TO CHALLENGE RACISM IN THEIR OWN COMMUNITIES. AFRICAN AMERICANS HAD THE RIGHT TO FORM THEIR OWN SEPARATE ORGANIZATIONS AND WERE FULLY JUSTIFIED IN NOT TRUSTING WHITES.

An SDS Journal of American Radicalism

RADICAL AMERICA

I WAS DETERMINED TO STAY SUSPENDED BETWEEN BLACK AND WHITE WORLDS AND SHARE WHAT I LEARNED FROM HISTORY WITH ANYONE WHO WANTED TO LISTEN. HISTORY WOULD BE MY REFUGE, MY INSPIRATION, MY SHELTER IN THE STORM. "RADICAL AMERICA" MAGAZINE WAS MY OUTLET.

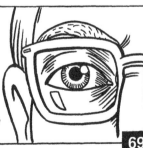

SO MUCH ABOUT THE OCCUPATION WAS **PRACTICAL.** WE WERE IN A GUERRILLA-LIKE SITUATION **PART OF THE TIME...**WE **NEEDED** TO HAVE A WET CLOTH FOR EVERYONE WHEN WE WOULD GET TEAR-GASSED. WE NEEDED TO TAKE **CARE OF A LOT** OF BUSINESSES, LIKE GETTING PEOPLE FED, MAKING SURE PEOPLE COULD STAY **CLEAN** – ALL OF **THAT** IN **ADDITION TO POLITICS.**

DIDN'T YOU **TWO** ACTUALLY GET **MARRIED** DURING THE **OCCUPATION?**

OH, **YES!** WE WERE ALREADY LIVING **TOGETHER** AND **PLANNING** TO GET MARRIED. IT WASN'T A DECISION MADE ON THE SPOT. BUT ON THIS **SUNDAY** NIGHT, THINGS WERE VERY **TENSE.** WE THOUGHT THAT **FAYERWEATHER** MIGHT CAPITULATE AND LEAVE THE **OTHER** BUILDINGS TO **FIGHT** IT **OUT.**

THE **PAGEANT PLAYERS** CAME AND DID A **PLAY** ABOUT THE KING AND QUEEN BEING **OVERTHROWN** BY THE PEOPLE. AND THERE WAS A **LOT OF DRUMMING,** PROBABLY BECAUSE THERE WERE A LOT OF **HIPPIES** IN **FAYERWEATHER,** TOO. THEY **BROUGHT** IN DRUMS.

THEN, AS **THIS** WAS GOING ON, A FRIEND OF OURS SAID, "THERE'S A **MOVE** TO GET YOU **TWO** MARRIED." AND WE SAID, "SURE, WHY THE **HELL** NOT!" THE CAMPUS **CHAPLIN, BILL STARR,** CLIMBED IN ONE OF THE WINDOWS. MEANWHILE, SOMEBODY WENT OUT AND **GOT** ME A PAIR OF **WHITE** JEANS AND A **WHITE** SWEATER MY SIZE. AND I GOT LOADED UP WITH **ALL** THE JEWELRY THAT **ANYBODY** HAD IN THE PLACE.

IT WAS A **BLACK POWER** PIN, WITH A BUNCH OF **LOVE** BEADS.

COPS AND THE COUNTERMAN JUMPED THE STUDENTS, COPS WAVING CLUBS.

THE STUDENTS OVERCAME THE COPS AND HELD THEM PEACEFULLY.

FOUR POLICE CARS PULLED UP IN FRONT, AND TEN OFFICERS CHARGED IN THE DOOR, GUNS DRAWN.

IT WAS OO MUCH...

THEY THREW THE STUDENTS ON THE FLOOR AND CUFFED THEM.

71

AT THE STATION HOUSE, POLICE **RAGED**: IT'S AN **INSULT** TO THE FORCE...THE STUDENT WHO OVERWHELMED A COP WAS **TIED** TO A **CHAIR** AND BEATEN.

WE OUGHT-TA SHOOT YOU RIGHT **NOW!**

WHAP

OTHER STUDENTS FACED THE SQUADROOM **WALL** WHILE MEMBERS OF THE PRECINCT **WHACKED** LEGS AND ELBOWS WITH **BLACKJACKS** AND **NIGHTSTICKS** AND AIMED **DROPKICKS** AT THEIR **BACKS.**

UNNH!

UGH!

KICK

YOU **FUCKING** ASSHOLES!

WE ELEVEN WERE **HANDCUFFED** TOGETHER IN A **SMALL** CELL, BEATEN BUT UNBOWED, **SINGING** OLD ROCK 'N' ROLL SONGS **TOGETHER,** FROM DOOWOP TO THE **STONES** AND BEATLES.

WE WERE **TOLD** THAT WE WERE CHARGED WITH FELONIOUS ASSAULT, WHICH CARRIED A **20-YEAR** SENTENCE. THE GUY WHO TOOK THE COP'S GUN **AWAY** WAS **CHARGED** WITH ROBBERY AND ATTEMPTED **MURDER**...THE **HEAVIEST** CHARGE AGAINST ANY **NEW YORK** SDS MEMBER.

IN ONE HOLDING CELL, SEVERAL WERE SURROUNDED...

WHAT ARE YOU DOING?

YOU ARE NOT SUPPOSED TO BE HERE!

THE PEOPLE IN HERE ARE GOD'S LOST CHILDREN. YOU CAN'T HELP THEM.

ALONE IN A CROWD...

AS SOON AS I GOT OUT OF JAIL I CALLED RUTHIE IN GEORGIA, WHO WAS AT HOME TAKING CARE OF HER FATHER...

RUTHIE...

MARK, HE'S DYING OF CANCER.

RUTH AND I DRIFTED APART, SO I THREW MYSELF INTO YET MORE ACTIVISM ON THE "CROSS BRONX EXPRESS," A COMMUNITY NEWSPAPER COVERING ANTI-WAR DEMOS AND WOMEN'S HEALTH ISSUES AND PROMPTING STRIKES AT HIGH SCHOOLS AND NEARBY COLLEGES.

BULLETIN

The Bronx Coalition has a regular schedul... meetings, workshops and informal get-togeth... our storefront at 109 E. 184th Street. The foll... is a general calendar. If you are interested in a... of the events, call the office at 933-2456 for information.

MONDAY MORNINGS — 10 to 12 — coffee hour for women to discuss women's liberation.

MONDAY EVENINGS — 8 pm — community Action Project — open to Bronx people interested in organizing around community issues — transit, rent-control, drugs, etc.

8 pm — meeting in homes to discuss health issues. Now working on setting up screening for pap smears and breast cancer detection tests out of storefront.

...EDNESDAY EVENINGS — 8 pm — Women's Liberation Meeting — open to new women — explain what we are beginning to do in different women's projects.

...URSDAY EVENINGS — 6:30 to 10 pm — Draft Counseling — scared of the draft? Now you can find out alternatives to going —

...IDAY EVENINGS — High School Meetings — open to all Bronx High School students — move against problems facing High School students; drugs, tracking, draft, civil rights, etc.

...DAY AFTERNOONS — 1 pm — Co...

Demo...

Re...

ANTI-IMPERIALIST ... with us ... Bronx.

ABORTION DEMONST... noon — 23... Bellevue Ho... Rally at 2... Demand"

EASTER BE-IN — March... — Look for ... in this society...

CITY-WIDE MARCH — ... 21 and All Po... by the Co... Committee an...

73

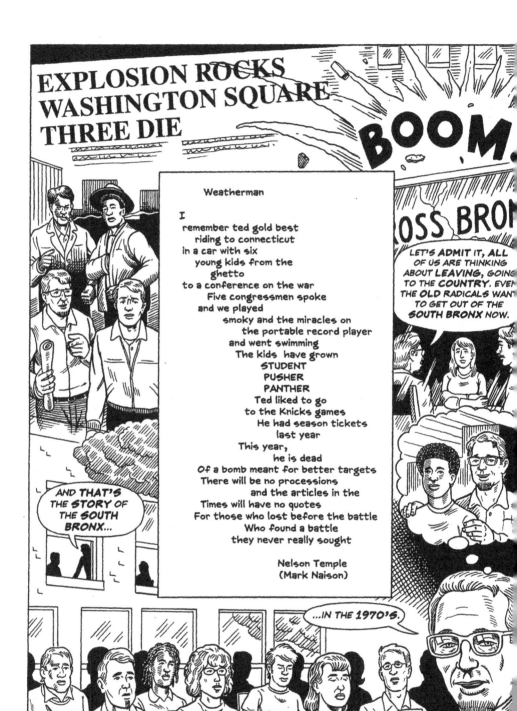

74

MY LIFE IN SDS

AS TOLD BY
PENELOPE ROSEMONT
ART BY **GARY DUMM**

MY FAMILY WERE **BOHEMIAN** OLD-SETTLERS ARRIVING IN **CHICAGO** IN **1859**. TEAMSTERS, PRINTERS, CARPENTERS, TAILORS, BAKERS, AND SHOPKEEPERS. ENERGETIC, THEY **FORMED** LODGES, JOINED UNIONS, AND **WENT** ON STRIKE. SOME WERE **BEATEN** BY POLICE AT McCORMICK'S JUST PRIOR TO **HAYMARKET** IN **1886**.

McCORMICK'S, MAY 3, 1886

POLICE PATROL

MY GRANDFATHER **KREKULE** WAS A **PRINTER** WHO HAD HIS **OWN** SHOP, AND LATER WORKED AS A **PRESSMAN** IN A **LARGE** PLANT. HE DIED BEFORE I WAS BORN, BUT WAS **REMEMBERED** FOR **3 SAYINGS**:

NEVER **JOIN** THE **NATIONAL GUARD**...YOU MIGHT HAVE **TO KILL YOUR BROTHER!**

YOU'RE **NOT A REAL AMERICAN** UNTIL YOU'VE SEEN **JAIL** FROM THE **INSIDE.**

DON'T BUY **MUTUAL FUNDS** – YOU CAN **LOSE** EVERYTHING.

STILL GOOD ADVICE!

MY DAD, **FRANK BARTIK,** WOKE ME UP **EACH** MORNING WITH A **SONG** – LATER I LEARNED THEY WERE **WOBBLY** SONGS. I'D **PRETEND** TO BE **ASLEEP** SO HE WOULD **SING** LONGER...

"HOLD THE FORT FOR **WE ARE COMING!**"

"THEY GO **WILD,** SIMPLY **WILD** OVER ME!"

MY MOM, **MAMIE**, A FEMININE-TYPE **WOMAN** WHO LOVED TO CROCHET AND BAKE AND MADE **DELIRIOUSLY** GOOD **DOUGHNUTS**, SINGLE-HANDEDLY **REROOFED** THE KITCHEN. HER **MOTTO** HAD **ALWAYS** BEEN:

IF HE CAN **DO** IT, I CAN **DO** IT!

HER **FAVORITE** KID'S STORY WAS "**THE LITTLE RED HEN**": I PLANTED IT, I WATERED IT, I BAKED IT, I'LL EAT IT! WITH A CAST OF **RELATIVES** LIKE THIS, IT'S **NOT** SURPRISING I TURNED OUT **BADLY.**

IN **1963** I **WENT** OFF TO **COLLEGE** TO STUDY **CHEMISTRY.** MY CAREER AS A **CHEM MAJOR** WAS **OVER** AFTER A CHAT WITH THE **HEAD** OF THE DEPARTMENT.

YOU HAVE TO **CHOOSE** BETWEEN **CHEMISTRY** AND GOING TO THE **ANTINUCLEAR WAR** DEMONSTRATION IN **WASHINGTON.**

WELL, I **GUESS** IT'S **GOOD-BYE!**

I TRANSFERRED TO ROOSEVELT UNIVERSITY. THE FIRST PERSON I MET WAS FRANKLIN ROSEMONT.

SO WHAT DO YOU DO?

I WORK ON THE REVOLUTION.

WE'RE GETTING READY TO OPEN AN ANARCHIST BOOKSHOP CALLED SOLIDARITY. WANT TO SEE IT?

THE GROUP AT THE BOOKSHOP PUBLISHED A MAGAZINE, "REBEL WORKER." THE CURRENT ISSUE FEATURED AN ARTICLE ON A BLUEBERRY PICKERS STRIKE THEY HAD ORGANIZED IN MICHIGAN. IT WAS MIMEOED.

THIS STENCIL MIGHT HOLD FOR ANOTHER TWO HUNDRED. THE "REBEL WORKER" IS AN IWW JOURNAL BUT WILL BE AIMED AT YOUNG PEOPLE — WITH UNINHIBITED CLASS-WAR HUMOR!

The Rebel Worker
Published periodically by the Chicago GMU Branch of the · Industrial Workers of the World ·

IN 1966 FRANKLIN AND I WENT TO FRANCE AND MET ANDRÉ BRETON AND THE SURREALIST GROUP, GUY DEBORD, AND M. KHAYATI. IN LONDON WE VISITED FREEDOM PRESS, THE SOLIDARITY GROUP, AND CHARLES RADCLIFFE.

HERE WE ARE VIEWING A SURREALIST OBJECT, "THE CONSUMER."

77

WE THOUGHT THAT SDS WAS JUST A MUSHY STUDENT GROUP TILL **SOLIDARITY BOOKSHOP** SET UP A TABLE AT **ROOSEVELT UNIVERSITY.** AN **RU** OFFICIAL STOPPED AT OUR TABLE.

IWW

ONE BIG UNION!

THE "TRIBUNE" WANTS TO FILM, SO GET THAT **COMMIE** STUFF **OUT OF HERE!** YOU'RE NOT STUDENTS ANYMORE; WE'LL HAVE YOU **ARRESTED FOR TRESPASSING!**

DON'T MOVE!

STEVE BAUM, RU SDS AT YOUR SERVICE!

IF THEY **TRY** TO KICK YOU OUT, WE'LL SHUT THE PLACE **DOWN!** WE'LL HAVE **1,000** PEOPLE HERE, SITTING IN! FILM THAT!

A LEAFLET WE DID AT **SOLIDARITY** CAUSED A **STIR** IN THE NEIGHBORHOOD AND **RILED** THE IWW OLD-TIMERS, TOO...

DROP-OUT

REVOLUTION

THE VERY **FIRST** PROPERTIES CONDEMNED BY **URBAN RENEWAL** WERE **SOLIDARITY BOOKSHOP, NORTHSIDE SDS,** AND **ALICE'S RESTAURANT.**

SOLIDARI BOOKSHO

THIS PROPERTY IS CONDEMNED

CITY OF CHICAGO

NOW

KEEP OUT

WE WENT TO SDS'S LIBERATION PRESS TO HAVE OUR FIRST SURREALIST BOOK, "THE MORNING OF A MACHINE GUN," PRINTED. OTHER PRINTERS HAD REFUSED TO PRINT IT. ONE SAID HE'D DO IT FOR $20,000. BEFORE PHOTOCOPYING, FREEDOM OF SPEECH MEANT OWNING A PRINTING PRESS.

THIS ANTIQUE PRESS HAS PROBLEMS!

WE'LL PRINT IT, BUT WE'RE PRETTY BUSY!

franklin rosemont

The MORNING

of

MACH

IN THE NEXT ROOM I WAS SURPRISED TO FIND MICHAEL JAMES, WHO I KNEW FROM OUR JACOBIN CLUB AT LFC. HE HAD BEEN PART OF THE BERKELEY FREE SPEECH STRUGGLE AND WAS NOW AN SDS ORGANIZER.

New Left Notes

THIS IS A GREAT ISSUE. WE'LL BE ABLE TO GET IT OUT ALL OVER THE PLACE!

SOON I HAD JOINED AND BEGAN TO HELP WITH PRINTING AND COLLATING – WE COULD NOT KEEP ENOUGH PAMPHLETS IN STOCK.

NEW RADICALS

PORT HURON STATEMENT

HUEY NEWTON

WHAT IS SDS?

THE CHAPTERS REQUESTED THEM BY THE HUNDREDS.

BLACK PANTHERS AND FOLKS FROM AIM CAME TO ADMIRE THE PRINT SHOP AND LEARN ABOUT PRINTING. IT WAS THE ONLY RADICAL PRINT SHOP IN THE COUNTRY EXCEPT FOR FREDY PERLMAN'S BLACK AND RED IN DETROIT.

THE FIRST POSTER OF THE **SURREALIST** GROUP WAS PRINTED BY **LIBERATION PRESS.** PEOPLE LOVED IT AND WANTED TO MEET **RENÉ CREVEL*** – WHO, ALTHOUGH HE WAS **"RIGHT ON,"** WAS ALSO UNFORTUNATELY LONG DEAD.

AU GRAND JOUR

The time is coming when seas of boiling rage will reverse the icy current of rivers, overflow and fertilize, fathoms deep, a crusted, petrified soil, tear away frontiers, uproot churches, clear the hills of bourgeois comp... ... decay... headlands of aristocratic insensitivi... obstacles the exploiting minority set in the wa... of the mass of the exploited, restore humanity... its future by freeing it from outdated instituti... religious fears, jingoistic mysticism and ... ... consecrates the evils

WOW! THAT RENÉ CREVEL SURE IS **"RIGHT ON!"** SOME GAL!

* HERE IN **AMERICA** RENÉ WAS CONSIDERED A **GIRL'S NAME.** NOT SO IN **FRANCE.**

DURING THE M.L. KING RIOTS AN **ENTIRE BLOCK** OF BUILDINGS **TWO** BLOCKS FROM THE **SDS** OFFICE WAS **BURNED** TO THE GROUND. WHEN I ARRIVED AT **SDS** THE NEXT DAY I ASKED WHAT ALL THE PEOPLE WERE DOING AT **WOOLWORTH'S** – I HAD **EXPECTED** IT TO BE **CLOSED,** BUT THERE WERE TWO **ORDERLY** LINES, ONE IN AND ONE OUT.

WHAT ARE THEY DOING?

LOOTING.

WOOLWORTH'S HAD BECOME A **FREE STORE.**

DURING THE **RIOTS** WE WENT OVER TO THE **BLACK** NEIGHBORHOOD IN A BEAT-UP, OPEN **PICK-UP** TRUCK. THERE WERE **POLICE** BARRICADES ALL OVER, BUT WE GOT **AROUND** THEM.

RIGHT ON!

WE SAW A **SHELL** OIL SIGN THAT HAD BEEN **TRANS-FORMED** APPROPRIATELY BY THE LOCALS TO READ **"HELL."**

SDS PRINTED **THOUSANDS** OF LEAFLETS FOR THE **APRIL 27** ANTIWAR DEMONSTRATION AND **DROPPED** PEOPLE OFF ON ALL THE MAIN DOWNTOWN CORNERS JUST BEFORE LUNCHTIME. THERE WERE **RUMORS** THAT THE **POLICE** WERE IN AN **EDGY MOOD** – TOO **TRUE**.

SOLIDARITY BOOKSHOP GROUP AND SOME OF THE SDS PRINTERS HAD FORMED THE **LOUIS LINGG*** MEMORIAL CHAPTER OF **SDS**.

ANARCHIS

ABOLISH THE DRAFT

BRING THE TROOPS HOME

OUT OF VIETNAM

* LOUIS LINGG WAS THE YOUNGEST OF THE HAYMARKET MARTYRS....AT HIS TRIAL HE SAID, "I HATE YOUR STATE – KILL ME FOR IT!"

UNPROVOKED, THE POLICE ATTACKED THE DEMONSTRATION (WE WERE ON STATE STREET UNDER A VERY GRAND THEATER MARQUEE). FRED ROGERS CHARGED THE POLICE – HE SURVIVED BUT WAS ARRESTED.

BLACK FLAGS TO THE FRONT!

STATE LAK

ACROSS THE STREET COMMUTERS WAITED. THEY WERE ADDRESSED BY DENNY ANCREM, WHO HAD LEAPED TO THE TOP OF A CAR AND POINTED TOWARD THE THEATER ACROSS THE STREET.

LADIES AND GENTLEMEN!...THIS IS AMERICA!

SOMEONE BEGAN TO SMASH PLATE GLASS WINDOWS – THIS FINALLY DISTRACTED THE POLICE FROM BEATING THE DEMONSTRATORS.

KRISH!

83

THERE WERE **SDS** STUDENT STRIKES AND SIT-INS COAST TO COAST – **COLUMBIA** UNIVERSITY TO **SAN FRANCISCO STATE**...AS WELL AS **ROOSEVELT** UNIVERSITY AND UNIVERSITY OF **CHICAGO**. A U. OF C. **SDS** SIT-IN FENDED OFF AMERICAN **NAZIS** BY THROWING **TYPEWRITERS** AT THEM.

PUBLISHED IN **MADISON**, "**RADICAL AMERICA**" WAS THE THEORETICAL JOURNAL OF **SDS**. FRANKLIN AND I WENT UP TO MEET **PAUL AND MARI JO BUHLE, MARK NAISON, MARTHA SONNENBERG**, ETC., AND PLOT AND SCHEME ON A BEAUTIFUL SUMMER DAY UNDER THE TREES.

WE CAN PUT TOGETHER A **SURREALIST** ISSUE...

WE'RE TOTALLY OUT OF ISSUE #1!

HAVE YOU MET D.A. LEVY, THE POET, YET?

LET'S DO ONE ON WOMEN BY WOMEN...

ENOUGH TALK...LET'S SMOKE SOME DOPE!

SOME OF THE **LEFT'S** GREAT YOUNG INTELLECTUALS **MEETING**.

HERBERT MARCUSE WAS THE MOST **IMPORTANT** THEORETICIAN OF THE TIME. WE WERE VERY **INFLUENCED** BY HIS BOOKS.

SURREALISM AS AN IDEA HAS NOT YET EXHAUSTED ITS **PROMISE** FOR THE FUTURE!

EROS AND CIVILIZATION

CRITIQUE OF PURE TOLERANCE

SDS'S NATIONAL OFFICE BEGAN TO PLAN FOR THE **DEMOCRATIC NATIONAL CONVENTION.** IT SET UP MOVEMENT CENTERS, ORGANIZED **FIRST AID** WORKERS, INVITED ITS ORGANIZERS TO **COME.**

RENÉ DAVIS APPEARED AT A **FRIDAY** STAFF MEETING AT THE **SDS** OFFICE. HE HAD AN **INTERESTING** PROPOSITION.

THE **CIA** IS WILLING TO PAY **SDS $10,000** TO **DISRUPT** THE CONVENTION.

HOW DO YOU **KNOW** IT'S THE **CIA?**

TELL 'EM TO KEEP THEIR **FILTHY** MONEY... WE'LL **DISRUPT** IT FREE OF **CHARGE!**

WHEN THE **DEMOCRATIC NATIONAL CONVENTION** BEGAN IN **CHICAGO,** THE **SDS** PRINT SHOP DID A **DAILY** TWO-SIDED WALL POSTER TO LET PEOPLE KNOW THE **REAL** NEWS. IT WAS **WIDELY** DISTRIBUTED AND **POSTED** UP WITH WALLPAPER PASTE ON THE MANY **URBAN RENEWAL** SITES.

ON THE **FIRST** NIGHT OF THE CONVENTION: WHILE **ALLEN GINSBERG** "OM"ED IN THE BACKGROUND, WE **LINKED** ARMS AND LED THE PEOPLE **OUT** OF THE PARK ON A MARCH DOWN **WELLS STREET** AND THROUGH MOST OF THE **NORTH SIDE** UNTIL WE WERE STOPPED AT A **CHICAGO RIVER** BRIDGE.

OOOOOOOOMMMMM!

IF YOU WERE GOING TO BE **CLUBBED,** IT MIGHT AS WELL HAPPEN **WHERE** PEOPLE COULD **SEE** IT. WE **ESCAPED** BEFORE THE **POLICE** COULD CLUB **EVERYONE** IN THE DARK.

85

THE PRINT SHOP WOULD **WORK** LATE INTO THE NIGHT TO BE **READY** FOR THE NEXT DAY. ONE NIGHT **FRANKLIN** HEARD A KNOCK AT OUR **BARRICADED** DOOR:

ALABAMA SDS...

...DON'T LAUGH!

MICHAEL JAMES DESIGNED A **POSTER** AND WE PRINTED IT. LATE THAT NIGHT, JUST AS WE WERE GETTING INTO THE CAR WITH **HUNDREDS** OF THEM TO **DROP OFF** AT MOVEMENT CENTERS, WE WERE **STOPPED** BY THE POLICE...

COULD I HAVE **ONE**?

HOT TOWN PIGS IN THE ST

MAKE IT TWO!

WE WERE SURPRISED THAT THEY **ONLY** ASKED FOR POSTERS AND SIMPLY LET US **GO**! WE'VE ALWAYS **WONDERED** WHAT THEY DID WITH THE POSTERS.

SDS GOT A CALL FROM **RADIO HAVANA**! THE PERSON ANSWERING THE PHONE WAS A BIT TOO **OPTIMISTIC**...

THE REVOLUTION IS NEARLY AT HAND!

HACK!

COFF!

CHOKE!

THE POLICE **BROKE UP** OUR MEETING IN **GRANT PARK**. THEY THREW **TEAR GAS** CANNISTERS, WE PICKED THEM UP AND THREW THEM **BACK**: THE POLICE HADN'T TAKEN INTO ACCOUNT THE **WIND** OFF THE **LAKE**, SO THEY TEARGASSED **THEMSELVES**.

DEMONSTRATORS SOUGHT A VIEW AND **SAFETY** ATOP A **STATUE** OF CIVIL WAR **GENERAL LOGAN** AND HIS HORSE. IT WAS **LOGAN'S** MOST FAMOUS MOMENT **SINCE THE CIVIL WAR.** AGAIN, **POLICE** WERE **NOT AMUSED!**

MIKE KLONSKY, SDS'S NATIONAL SECRETARY, ORGANIZED US INTO **SMALL GROUPS** FOR **SAFETY** AND STRATEGIC **REASONS.** AND WHEN THE **POLICE** BROKE UP OUR **LATE-NIGHT** MARCHES, OUR GROUPS HEADED OFF IN **DIFFERENT** DIRECTIONS... WE (AND THE **COPS**) GOT **PLENTY** OF EXERCISE, BUT WE **AVOIDED** BEING HURT.

THEY'VE TURNED...LET'S RUN FOR IT!

ABBIE HOFFMAN AND THE **YIPPIES** ADDED A **ZANY** QUALITY TO PUBLIC **EVENTS**...

TURN ON, TUNE IN, DROP OUT! **VOTE LSD!**

PIGASUS

CHICAGO'S MAYOR RICHARD DALEY CAME OUT WITH SO MANY GOOD **LINES** THAT A **BOOK** ENTITLED "QUOTATIONS FROM CHAIRMAN DALEY" WAS PUBLISHED. **LOCALLY,** AT LEAST, IT WAS A **BESTSELLER.**

THE **POLICE** ARE NOT HERE TO **PREVENT** DISORDER, THEY ARE HERE TO **PRESERVE** DISORDER!

87

THE DEMOCRATIC CONVENTION DEMONSTRATIONS GOT GREAT PUBLICITY – LARGELY BECAUSE THE POLICE HAD ALSO CLUBBED THE PRESS AS "THE WHOLE WORLD WAS WATCHING."

I'M WITH CBS!

LAWRENCE LIPTON LATER DIED DUE TO INJURIES HE RECEIVED.

IN THE FALL OF '68 OUR SURREALIST GALLERY – GALLERY BUGS BUNNY – WAS A HIT WITH NEIGHBORHOOD DROPOUTS AND SDS AS WELL. IT WAS WRITTEN UP IN THE "TRIBUNE," BUT EVERY TIME FRANKLIN OR GREEN USED THE WORD "IMPERIALISM" THEY CHANGED IT TO "MATERIALISM"!

SDS LATER PUBLISHED A PAMPHLET ON WORKING. FRANKLIN'S MOM, WHO WORKED IN THE MARSHALL FIELDS FOUNDATION DEPARTMENT (BRAS AND GIRDLES), WAS CALLED TO A BRIEF DEPARTMENTAL MEETING WHERE HER BOSS INFORMED HER THAT SDS WAS PLANNING TO SUBVERT THE FOUNDATION DEPARTMENT...

FOUNDATION DEPARTMENT

SO BE ON THE LOOKOUT FOR ANY YOUNG EMPLOYEES YOU MIGHT THINK ARE SDSERS.

THE 1969 SDS CONVENTION WAS AT THE COLISEUM, FORMER HOME OF THE "FRIDAY NIGHT FIGHTS" AND LIBBY PRISON. HINKY DINK HELD GRAND BALLS THERE. IT WAS A FIELD DAY FOR EGOS AND POLICE AGENTS – SAD TO REALIZE THAT A TASTE OF POWER HAD CORRUPTED SDS, AND THAT PEOPLE WOULD DESTROY SO EASILY WHAT HAD BEEN BUILT WITH SUCH GREAT EFFORT...

ANARCHISTS WROTE IN "FREEDOM PRESS": "THEY'RE ALL CRAZY!"

An SDS Journal of American Radicalism

RADICAL AMERICA

SPECIAL ISSUE

SurRealism

in the service of the

Revolution

JANUARY, 1970
75¢

WE PREPARED A SURREALIST ISSUE OF "RADICAL AMERICA" THAT WENT TO PRESS IN '69, AND FINALLY APPEARED IN 1970. IT WAS THE LAST TO CALL ITSELF AN SDS JOURNAL. CRAMMED FULL OF GREAT TEXTS, IT WOULD GET A LOT OF RESPONSE – PRO AND CON. THE NUMBER OF PEOPLE BECOMING RADICALIZED CONTINUED TO GROW, BUT SDS WAS NO LONGER THERE TO JOIN AND UNITE THEM!

THERE WAS A DJ BACK THEN WHO WOULD CLOSE HIS SHOW WITH THE FOLLOWING ADMONITION:

WELL, FOLKS, IF YOU DON'T LIKE THE NEWS TODAY, GO OUT AND MAKE SOME OF YOUR OWN!

ALSO GOOD ADVICE!

89

"FILL-IN" LeBLANC

STORY BY PAUL LeBLANC & PAUL BUHLE

ART BY GARY DUMM

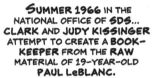

SUMMER 1966 IN THE NATIONAL OFFICE OF SDS... CLARK AND JUDY KISSINGER ATTEMPT TO CREATE A BOOK-KEEPER FROM THE RAW MATERIAL OF 19-YEAR-OLD PAUL LeBLANC.

SHIT!

HELL!

DAMN!

HOWZIT GOING, PAUL?

WE NEED IT DONE AND YOU CAN DO IT. BESIDES, THERE ARE MORE NEW CHAPTERS OF SDS EVERY MONTH!

CLARK...YOU THINK I CAN LEARN HOW TO DO THIS?

AND MORE EXPENSES.

WHAT IF THERE ISN'T ANY BUDGET TO BALANCE?

WE'LL ASK OUR LIBERAL FRIENDS FOR SOME MORE MONEY... AND WE HAVE THE PHIL OCHS CONCERT IN A FEW WEEKS...

END

IT'S A LONG WAY TO HAZARD

STORY & ART BY NICK THORKELSON

On the spring of 1964 Johnny Bancroft, Jane Ehrlich, and I decided to attend a student/miner conference in Hazard, Kentucky.

WE CAN GET A RIDE TO LOUISVILLE AND HITCH FROM THERE.

RIDES

"BOOK SACK" (BACKPACKS HAD NOT CAUGHT ON YET)

THE CONFERENCE WAS ORGANIZED BY SDS'S ECONOMIC RESEARCH AND ACTION PROJECT (ERAP) & THE COMMITTEE FOR MINERS.

A LITTLE BACKGROUND:

IN 1962–63, UNEMPLOYED MINERS OF HAZARD, KY, FOUGHT THE PROLIFERATION OF NONUNION "TRUCK MINES" WITH MILITANT ROVING PICKETS.

HEY!

EEK!

POW!

BAP!

YOW!

THOK!

WACK!

OUCH!

DESPITE OPPOSITION FROM LOCAL POLICE, MEDIA, POLITICIANS, & MERCHANTS, THEY HAD SOME SUCCESS DISRUPTING MINES, SO THE OPERATORS CALLED IN THE FBI. WHEN EIGHT MINERS WERE INDICTED FOR CONSPIRACY, THE COMMITTEE FOR MINERS WAS SET UP TO COORDINATE LEGAL DEFENSE, RELIEF, AND PUBLICITY.

BUT THE UNIONS WOULDN'T HELP BECAUSE THE MINEWORKERS' UNION (UMWA) HADN'T AUTHORIZED THE STRIKE—

A.F.L. C.I.O.

NO ROOM AT THIS INN

AND THE FEDS WOULDN'T HELP BECAUSE THEY COULDN'T OFFEND THE LOCAL DEMOCRATIC PARTY MACHINE—

NOR THIS ONE

THE ONLY GROUP THAT WANTED TO PITCH IN WAS:

SDS

ONE MANGER AVAIL. IMMEDIATELY FOR BIRTH OF INTERRACIAL MOVEMENT OF THE POOR

IN THOSE DAYS YOU WOULD COME HOME FROM A DEMONSTRATION OR CONFERENCE WITH A PILE OF THOUGHTFUL MIMEOGRAPHED DOCUMENTS.

I JUST FOUND A GOOD ONE FROM THE HAZARD CONFERENCE.

RICHARD GREENBERG'S "PROBLEMS RELATING TO UNEMPLOYMENT IN THE VICINITY OF HAZARD, KENTUCKY"* MAKES IT CLEAR THAT THE MINERS' REBELLION OF 1962-64 WAS A DOOMED EFFORT TO REGAIN THE LOST GROUND OF INDUSTRIAL UNIONISM IN APPALACHIA.

UNION COMPROMISES

DECLINE OF NORTHERN INDUSTRY

AUTOMATION

HOME HEATING OIL

DIESEL FUEL

FALLING PRICE OF COAL

AS FOR THE GOALS OF SDS/ERAP: MOST OF THE INDICTED MINERS WERE ACQUITTED. NEW FEDERAL PROGRAMS DID PROVIDE SOME JOBS & INCOME SUPPORTS. BUT ATTEMPTS TO ELECT A PRO-MINER SHERIFF AND HOSPITAL BOARD FAILED. ERAP CLOSED DOWN ITS HAZARD PROJECT THE FOLLOWING FALL.

TORKTUBES! YOU'RE BACK! DIDJA CHANGE THE WORLD?

DIDJA MEET ANY POVERTS?

WHAT ERAP CHANGED WAS OUR MINDS— WE CAME TO SEE POVERTY NOT AS A PATHOLOGY OR AN URBAN OR A RACE THING BUT AS A DIRECT CONSEQUENCE OF CAPITALIST SOCIAL RELATIONS.

I'D STILL LIKE TO SEE THAT INTERRACIAL MOVEMENT OF THE POOR, THOUGH!

END

NICK THORKELSON

* GREENBERG'S PAPER IS ONLINE AT www.educationanddemocracy.org/FSCpdf/CurryTextOnlyPart2.pdf; OTHER SOURCES: ARTICLES BY HAMISH SINCLAIR & PETER WILEY IN RADICAL AMERICA AND STUDIES ON THE LEFT, AND INTERVIEWS WITH PETER WILEY & STANLEY ARONOWITZ. PETER WAS PART OF THE HAZARD ERAP PROJECT; HAMISH & STANLEY LED THE COMMITTEE FOR MINERS. THIS COMIC IS FOR JANE EHRLICH, 1945-80.

95

CLEVELAND ERAP PROJECT

STORY BY ALAN WALD
AND HARVEY PEKAR
ART BY GARY DUMM

IN LATE JANUARY 1966 ALAN WALD, A NINETEEN-YEAR-OLD LIT MAJOR FROM ANTIOCH COLLEGE, ARRIVED IN CLEVELAND TO JOIN SDS'S ECONOMIC RESEARCH AND ACTION PROJECT (ERAP) WHILE WORKING AT A COOPERATIVE JOB AS A CHILD CARE WORKER AT CLEVELAND METRO GENERAL HOSPITAL.

HE WAS A POLITICAL NOVICE, MORE INTERESTED IN THE BEAT WRITERS AND WILLIAM BLAKE THAN POLITICS, BUT HE HAD BEEN ATTRACTED TO SDS'S COMMUNITY ORGANIZING EFFORTS AND ITS CALL FOR AN INTERRACIAL MOVEMENT OF THE POOR. TOO YOUNG AND ILL-INFORMED TO HAVE PARTICIPATED IN THE SOUTHERN CIVIL RIGHTS MOVEMENT, HE SAW ERAP AS A CHANCE TO MAKE A CONTRIBUTION TO THE NEW MOVEMENTS IN THE NORTH AGAINST RACISM AND POVERTY.

KEROUAC

BLAKE

WITH HIS POLITICALLY SOPHISTICATED GIRLFRIEND, CELIA STODOLA, WHO HAD BEEN AN ANTIWAR RADICAL SINCE HIGH SCHOOL IN NORTH DAKOTA, HE HAD MADE ARRANGEMENTS TO LIVE WITHIN A BLOCK OF THE ERAP HOUSE ON CLEVELAND'S NEAR WEST SIDE.

ANTIOCH WORK-STUDY STUDENTS HAD BEEN AFFILIATING WITH THE CLEVELAND PROJECT SINCE IT BEGAN IN EARLY 1964, ORIGINALLY AT THE SUGGESTION OF MEDICAL STUDENTS OLIVER FEIN AND CHARLOTTE PHILLIPS. MOST OF THESE SHORT-TERM RESIDENTS WERE ASKED TO JOIN THE NEAR WEST SIDE PROJECT IN A NEIGHBORHOOD THAT WAS A COMBINATION OF MIGRANTS FROM APPALACHIA AND EASTERN EUROPE AND A GROWING NUMBER OF PUERTO RICANS.

UNEMPLOYMENT IN THE NEIGHBOR-
HOOD WAS UP TO **20%** AND HOUS-
ING WAS SO **BAD** THAT **ALAN** AND
CELIA'S APARTMENT HAD **CRACKS**
IN THE WALL AND **BROKEN** WINDOWS
WHERE THE WINTER **COLD** POURED IN.
OFTEN DRUNKS WERE SLEEPING ON THE
FRONT **STEPS. COOKING,** MOSTLY
BEANS FROM CANS, WAS DONE ON A
HOT PLATE.

THEY ATTENDED **POLITICAL** MEETINGS AT THE **PROJECT
HOUSE,** WHICH WAS EXPLAINED TO THEM AS A DEMOCRATI-
CALLY RUN **COMMUNE.** MEN AND WOMEN PARTICIPATED
EQUALLY IN CLEANING, SHOPPING, AND COOKING, WITH A
GIGANTIC POT OF **SPAGHETTI** AS THE MOST FREQUENT DISH.

POLITICAL AND OTHER DECISIONS WERE CARRIED
OUT BY **CONSENSUS,** USUALLY PRECEDED BY
EXTRAORDINARILY **LONG** MEETINGS. SPECIAL
HEALTH **EXERCISES,** FEATURING RUNNING IN
PLACE, WERE DONE **DAILY.** BOOKS WERE PASSED
AROUND SUCH AS KEN KESEY'S **"SOMETIMES
A GREAT NOTION."**

BY THIS TIME THE **NEAR WEST SIDE** WAS LED BY
SHARON JEFFREY, KEN AND **CAROL
McELDOWNEY, PAUL POTTER,** AND **DAVID
STRAUSS. KATHY BOUDIN** LIVED NEARBY AND
WAS ASSIGNED TO MEET **PRIVATELY** WITH **ALAN**
AND **CELIA** TO **DISCUSS** THEIR WORK.

OCCASIONALLY
NATIONAL
LEADERS FROM
OTHER CITIES,
SUCH AS **TOM
HAYDEN,** PASSED
THROUGH TO
GIVE **REPORTS**
ON **POLITICAL**
MATTERS.

THE PRIMARY CONCERN OF THE **NEAR WEST SIDE** PROJECT WAS A **WELFARE RIGHTS** GROUP LED BY A LOCAL WOMAN, **LILLIAN CRAIG.** SHE IS MENTIONED IN ALL THE BOOKS AS THE **ONE** LOCAL **SUCCESS** STORY, A REAL **COMMUNITY** LEADER FOR WELFARE RIGHTS, ETC.

DUE TO HIS LITERARY INTERESTS, **ALAN** WAS **ASSIGNED** TO WORK WITH A **RADICAL THEATER** GROUP THAT RENTED A **STOREFRONT** IN THE COMMUNITY.

PLAYS WERE WRITTEN THAT WERE ROUGHLY MODELED ON **BRECHTIAN** STRATEGIES, WITH THE NAMES AND EVENTS **CHANGED** TO TAKE PLACE IN THE CLEVELAND COMMUNITY. AFTER WORK AT THE HOSPITAL AND ON WEEKENDS **ALAN** PARTICIPATED IN GROUP MEETINGS TO **COLLECTIVELY** PREPARE THE TEXTS AND STAGING, THEN **ACTED** IN THE SKITS. THESE WERE FOLLOWED BY DISCUSSIONS FROM THE **AUDIENCE,** WHICH WAS LARGELY PEOPLE IN THE COMMUNITY. THE RADICAL JOURNALIST **ANDREW KOPKIND** ATTENDED SOME OF THE PERFORMANCES AND **WROTE** ABOUT THEM IN **"THE NATION"**...

Theater Success

A series of one-act skits were presented at the Community Union Center on Wednesday, February 9. About forty people from the Near West Side were present. Each and every act had a message. Among them were acts pertaining to how a major treats a common man, how the price of living goes up but not the wages for the poor man. A hospital scene brought much discussion and also an act about the lost poor man in the U.S.

He was no longer poor but was "lower middle class." He was not happy because he had no say-so over the way he had been "re-made" by the "Great Society." This act also brought much discussion. The residents of the Near West Side that were present really understood what was being said. The Community Theater is directed by Bob Smiddie, who also writes the plays that are presented. Many bouquets to him. All of us that have seen any of Bob's plays hope to see more and more as time goes on.

END

HARVEY PEKAR ☆ JOIN CHICAGO ☆ SUMMER McCLINTON

ONE OF THE MOST SUCCESSFUL ERAP GROUPS WAS ONE CALLED "JOIN" (JOBS OR INCOME NOW) IN CHICAGO'S UPTOWN NEIGHBORHOOD WHICH WAS HEAVILY POPULATED BY POOR AND WORKING-CLASS WHITE MIGRANTS FROM THE SOUTH AND THEIR CHILDREN.

IT WAS ALSO PERHAPS THE LONGEST-LIVED ERAP, ENDING IN 1968, DUE PARTLY TO SDS'S EMPHASIS ON OTHER PROJECTS, SUCH AS THE ANTIWAR MOVEMENT.

HELLO, MR. WILBUR.

HEY, HI JIMMY.

DURING ITS RELATIVELY SHORT EXISTENCE, JOIN ACCOMPLISHED A GREAT DEAL, FROM HELPING RESIDENTS WITH SLUMLORDS TO JOB SEEKING.

YOU DON'T HAVE TO PUT UP WITH THAT STUFF FROM LANDLORDS.

THEY WORKED FOR WELFARE AND HOUSING IMPROVEMENT, DEALT WITH RIP-OFF LOCAL BUSINESSMEN, ORGANIZED THE UNEMPLOYED, AND HELPED EDUCATE RESIDENTS, SOME OF WHOM LEARNED TO READ IN THE PROCESS.

REMEMBER, "I" BEFORE "E" EXCEPT AFTER "C."

99

JOIN ALSO WORKED FOR WOMEN'S RIGHTS BEFORE IT BECAME A HIGH-VISIBILITY ISSUE.

WE'VE GOT TO MAKE PROGRESS TO GET ANTI-DISCRIMINATION LAWS PASSED.

HEY, KID, WHAT YOU DOING?

MELODY JAMES, SISTER OF HIGH-RANKING MEMBER MIKE JAMES, CAME IN AND SET UP A NEIGHBORHOOD GUERRILLA THEATER.

scene: 4 confrontation

THERE WAS TROUBLE WITH POLICE BRUTALITY IN THE UPTOWN NEIGHBORHOOD, AND JOIN TOOK A STAND AGAINST IT.

I'M NOT MAKIN' NO TROUBLE, WHY YOU HASSLING ME?

TAKE THAT!

IN REPLY THE POLICE PLANTED DRUGS IN THE JOIN OFFICE, THEN BROKE IN AND TRASHED IT.

AS A RESULT, JOIN CALLED FOR AN INDEPENDENT POLICE REVIEW BOARD, WHICH LED TO THE FORMATION OF A NEIGHBORHOOD ORGANIZATION CALLED CITIZEN ALERT, WHICH IS STILL INFLUENCING SIMILAR GROUPS TODAY.

KEEP AN EYE ON HIM.

JOIN HOPED TO EVOLVE A SHADOW PRECINCT ORGANIZATION AND ESTABLISHED BLOCK CLUBS AND TENANT GROUPS AS A BASIS FOR THIS.

MY RENT WAS ONE DAY LATE AND THEY TURNED OFF THE ELECTRICITY.

JOIN EVEN HAD A HAND IN NATIONAL POLITICS. THE PEACE AND FREEDOM PARTY'S CANDIDATE FOR VICE PRESIDENT IN 1968 WAS JOIN MEMBER PEGGY TERRY, AND MIKE JAMES AND OTHERS CAMPAIGNED IN HER BEHALF.

AND NOW, MEET THE NEXT VICE PRESIDENT OF THE USA, PEGGY TERRY!

HOW DOES THIS LOOK?

AFTER SDS BROKE INTO QUARRELING FACTIONS, IT GAVE UP ON THE IDEA OF ERAPS; BUT INDIVIDUAL JOIN MEMBERS STAYED IN THE CHICAGO AREA TO FORM NEW GROUPS AND START A PAPER, "RISING UP ANGRY," AND ORGANIZING. OTHERS GOT INVOLVED IN THE ANTIWAR MOVEMENT.

JOIN WAS PREVENTED FROM REALIZING ITS GOALS IMMEDIATELY,

BUT IT PLANTED SOME SEEDS.

...AND THE ROOTS ARE STILL THERE.

END

101

Phil Ochs demonstrated with
the demonstrators, articulated
their thoughts, and dreamed
aloud with and for them.

"I Ain't Marchin' Anymore"

PHIL OCHS, THE PROTEST SONG, AND SDS

Story & Layouts · John Pietaro
Pencils/Inks · Gary Dumm

BY 1965 THE FLEDGLING **ANTI-WAR** MOVEMENT BEGAN TO SHOW A MARKED **GROWTH.** ITS RANKS NOT ONLY GREW IN **NUMBERS** BUT IN VOLUME AS WELL...AND THE SOUNDTRACK WAS CREATED BY **PROTEST** SINGERS, CONTEMPORARIES OF THE STUDENTS, WHO WERE PART OF THE CONTINUUM OF THE **FOLK** REVIVAL THAT HAD SPAWNED THE **ALMANAC** SINGERS 20 YEARS BEFORE...

END THE WAR NOW

END WAR NOW

HELL NO!

1945...

SIS CUNNINGHAM

LEE HAYS

C.I.O.

MILLARD LAMPELL

C.I.O.

WOODY GUTHRIE

AND NOW, HERE'S ONE ABOUT THIS **DAMNED** ANTISTRIKE PLEDGE WE NEED TO **STAMP OUT!**

C.I.O.

PETE SEEGER

HOWEVER, THE FOLK MUSIC **BOOM** OF THE 1960'S ALLOWED TOPICAL SONGWRITERS TO HAVE THE **IDEAL** GENRE IN WHICH TO SING THE PRAISES OF **DISSENT.** MODERN PROTEST MUSIC RANG OUT ON COLLEGE CAMPUSES AND IN **COFFEEHOUSES** ALL OVER THE COUNTRY – AND BEYOND. THE FOLKIES IN **CREW CUTS** WHO SANG PERFECT 3-PART HARMONY GAVE WAY TO THE ROOTS OF THE MUSIC, AS SOCIAL **UNREST** REPLACED POLITE HUMOR. STILL, THE STAKES FOR COMMERCIAL SUCCESS WERE **HIGH** AND FEW OF THE **NEW** FOLKSINGERS DARED FOCUS **EXCLUSIVELY** ON THE **PROTEST** SONG...

ZENITH

RCA

HEY, MAN, NOT SINCE "FREEWHEELIN'" HAVE I HEARD ANYTHING LIKE THIS.

103

...BUT PHIL OCHS DID

WE CALL FOR NO WIDER WAR...

FREEDOM RIDES...

BUT THERE'S NO CHRISTMAS IN KENTUCKY...

I'LL SING YOU A SONG ABOUT JOHN HENRY FAULK...

TOO MANY MARTYRS AND TOO MANY DEATHS...

HERE COMES THE BIG PARADE...

OCHS REFUSED TO ACT SIMPLY AS TOWN CRIER. RATHER, HE BECAME ONE WITH THE ACTIVISTS, TRAVELING TO KENTUCKY TO SING FOR THE DESTITUTE, STRIKING MINERS AND THEN JOINING IN ON THE FREEDOM RIDES TO FIGHT FOR CIVIL RIGHTS. MISSISSIPPI, HE LEARNED IN 1964, WAS EVEN HOTTER THAN THE LABOR WARS OF KENTUCKY AND VIRGINIA. BUT THE BATTLE WAS JUST BEGINNING...

I JUST FEEL YOU DON'T UNDERSTAND. A PROTEST SONG CANNOT FUNCTION AS FILLER – IT'S SOMETHING SO SPECIFIC THAT YOU CAN'T MISTAKE IT FOR BULLSHIT. A PROTEST SONG IS SOMETHING YOU DON'T HEAR ON THE RADIO.

AS SDS PLANNED ITS FIRST LARGE-SCALE DEMONSTRATION IN WASHINGTON, D.C., OCHS, ALONG WITH JOAN BAEZ AND JUDY COLLINS, WAS A NECESSARY INGREDIENT. PHIL OCHS'S IMPORTANCE WENT WELL BEYOND MERE ENTERTAINMENT. HIS POWER AS A STORYTELLER, A TEACHER, AN INSPIRATION, AND AN AGITATOR BECAME INTEGRAL.

1965

BEFORE THE DAYS OF MASS MEDIA, THE FOLKSINGER WAS OFTEN A TRAVELING NEWSPAPER, SPREADING TALES THROUGH MUSIC.

THERE IS AN URGENT NEED FOR AMERICANS TO LOOK DEEPLY INTO THEMSELVES AND THEIR ACTIONS. MUSICAL POETRY IS PERHAPS THE MOST EFFECTIVE MIRROR AVAILABLE.

EVERY NEWSPAPER HEADLINE IS A POTENTIAL SONG.

THE MORNING OF APRIL 17, 1965: HUNDREDS UPON HUNDREDS OF PROTESTERS BEGAN TO ENGORGE THE AREA LEADING TOWARD WASHINGTON, D.C.'S PENNSYLVANIA AVENUE. BY NINE A.M., THE ORGANIZED BUT DISPARATE GROUP HAD SWELLED WELL INTO THE THOUSANDS.

BUSES ARRIVED FROM ALL POINTS SOUTH, WEST, EAST, AND NORTH, AND THE ENDORSEMENTS FROM A VAST COLLECTION OF PROGRESSIVE GROUPS LAID A STRONG FOUNDATION. THE ANTI-VIETNAM WAR MOVEMENT HAD ARRIVED, AND SDS WAS THE LIFE FORCE.

SDS
ERAP

Maine
Toronto for PEACE
STUDENT PEACE UNION
North Dakota
COMMITTEE for NON VIOLENT ACTION
North Texas State SDS
LOCAL 1199
YPSL
Youth Against WAR AND Fascism
Tulsa 4 PEACE
SNCC
Selma or SAIGON
One Student One VOTE
DuBois Clubs
WWP
MISSISSIPPI SDS
SANE
STUDENTS for a DEMOCRATIC SOCIETY
Minnesota SDS
WOMEN STRIKE for PEACE
WRL
SDS N.Y.
CPUSA

AS THE THRONGS MARCHED FORWARD, THEY WOULD DEVELOP INTO THE NATION'S LARGEST ANTIWAR DEMONSTRATION. THE FATES OFFERED UP NOT ONLY CLASSIC SOLIDARITY TO THE CAUSE BUT PERFECT RALLY WEATHER: SPRING, IN ALL ITS GLORY, SHONE ON THE DEMONSTRATORS, INDICATING THAT "THE GOOD FIGHT" WAS, INDEED, GOOD. ALL ROADS LED TOWARD THE RALLY SITE – THE OUTDOOR SYLVAN THEATER, IN THE SHADOW OF THE WASHINGTON MONUMENT.

105

AFTER THE PROTESTERS SANG A **POWERFUL** RENDITION OF **"WE SHALL OVERCOME,"** THE SONG THAT HAD CARRIED SO MANY THROUGH THE **BLOODY** BATTLES FOR THE RIGHTS OF **BLACK** AMERICANS, THE PROGRAM BEGAN. THE **VISCERAL** STRENGTH OF PROTEST MUSIC WAS FURTHER **EVIDENCED** BY THE PERFORMANCES OF **JOAN BAEZ, JUDY COLLINS,** AND...

END THE WAR NOW

...PHIL OCHS!

SDS

OCHS'S ACERBIC TONGUE WAS QUICK TO COMMENT ON THE **SPLIT** BETWEEN CLASSIC **LIBERALS** AND THE MORE ACTIVIST **RADICALS** IN THE MOVEMENT. NOT **ALL** UNDERSTOOD HIS **HUMOR.**

ONCE I WAS **YOUNG** AND IMPULSIVE, I WORE EVERY CONCEIVABLE **PIN,** EVEN WENT TO THE SOCIALIST MEETINGS, LEARNED **ALL** THE OLD UNION HYMNS...

...BUT I'VE GROWN OLDER AND WISER, THAT'S WHY I'M TURNING YOU IN...LOVE ME, LOVE ME, I'M A LIBERAL.

HEY! LIBERALISM IS **NOT** OUR ENEMY — THERE ARE **GOOD** LIBERALS AND **BAD** LIBERALS!!

I.F. STONE

BUT THE ONE **SONG** THAT REALLY SPOKE TO THE **YOUTH** MOVEMENT FOR PEACE, THAT ESTABLISHED ITS ANGER, PRIDE, AND DETERMINATION, ALSO MODELED RESISTANCE THROUGHOUT U.S. HISTORY.

OH, I **MARCHED** TO THE BATTLE OF **NEW ORLEANS** AT THE **END** OF THE EARLY BRITISH **WAR**...

...THE YOUNG LAND STARTED **GROWING,** THE YOUNG BLOOD STARTED **FLOWING,** BUT —

—I AIN'T **MARCHIN'** ANYMORE!

106

PAXTON

CARNEGIE HALL
Friday Evening, September 24, 1965
SING-IN FOR PEACE

Eric Anderson   Danny Kalb

Theodore Bikel   Chad Mitchel

BIKEL

SPONSORED BY THE FOLKSONG MAGAZINE **"SING OUT,"** THE **CARNEGIE HALL SING-IN FOR PEACE** WAS **HISTORIC,** NOT ONLY AS A VEHICLE FOR **PROTEST MUSIC** AND THE **NEW PEACE MOVEMENT,** BUT AS A MEETING GROUND FOR THE **OLD LEFT** AND THE **NEW LEFT...**

DAVIS

Oscar Brand   Tom Paxton

Barbara Dane   Ishmael Reed

Rev. Gary Davis   Bernice Reagon

Jack Elliot   e Seeger

Greenbriar Boys   edom Singers

JOHNSON

I STOLE **CALIFORNIA** FROM THE **MEXICAN** LAND, FOUGHT IN THE **BLOODY** CIVIL WAR...

...YES, I EVEN **KILLED** MY BROTHERS AND SO MANY **OTHERS,** BUT I **AIN'T** MARCHIN' ANYMORE!

BLUES AND FOLK MUSIC EASILY BLENDED INTO **POPULAR SONG** AND THE POETRY OF THE GREAT **REVOLUTIONARY** WRITER **BERTOLT BRECHT.**

...THEN I **MARCHED** TO THE BATTLE OF THE **GERMAN** TRENCH IN A **WAR** THAT WAS **BOUND** TO END **ALL WARS;** I MUST HAVE **KILLED** A **MILLION** MEN, BUT **NOW** THEY WANT ME BACK **AGAIN...**

THIS NIGHT WOULD SIGNAL THE DAWN OF THE MODERN **PEACE MOVEMENT,** WHICH WAS LED BY A **GENERATION** CAUGHT BETWEEN THE **FRIGHTENED FIFTIES** AND THE **PROMISE** OF A NEW DAY.

...**BUT I AIN'T MARCHIN' ANYMORE!**

BY MIDNIGHT THE CONCERT HAD **SPILLED** OUT ONTO THE STREET; **AUDIENCE** AND **PERFORMER** ALIKE LOCKED ARMS AND TOOK THE NIGHT AS THEIR **OWN.** THEIR DEFIANT BUT IMPROMPTU **PARADE** WALKED IN FORMATION FROM MID-TOWN **MANHATTAN** ALL THE WAY DOWN TO **GREENWICH VILLAGE,** THE **OFFICIAL** HOME OF THE **FOLK SCENE.** THEY HELD A **RALLY** IN **WASHINGTON SQUARE PARK** AT 4:09 A.M. PHIL OCHS WAS THERE.

IT'S ALWAYS THE OLD THAT **LEAD** US TO THE **WAR**; IT'S **ALWAYS** THE YOUNG WHO **FALL**. NOW LOOK AT ALL WE'VE **WON** WITH A SABRE AND A **GUN** – TELL ME: **IS IT WORTH IT ALL?!**

Though he was **LOVED** BY THE STUDENTS, **OCHS** CARRIED AN **INNER** LONELINESS WITH HIM THAT WAS **PERVASIVE**. PARALLEL TO THE STRUGGLE FOR GLOBAL **PEACE**, HIS **PERSONAL** CONFLICT WOULD BUILD TOWARD AN ERUPTION AND ULTIMATELY GROW COLD. EVEN IN **1965**, IN THE EARLY HOURS OF AN AUTUMN MORNING IN **WASHINGTON SQUARE**, ONE COULD HEAR THE **SADNESS** IN THIS TROUBADOUR OF A NEW **YOUTH** MOVEMENT, BUT FEW COULD HEAR A **SINGULAR** VOICE. THE LOUDEST VOICES WERE THOSE THAT SANG IN **UNISON**. STILL – **PHIL OCHS WAS THERE!**

"CALL IT PEACE OR CALL IT TREASON, CALL IT LOVE OR CALL IT REASON... BUT **I AIN'T MARCHIN'** ANYMORE."

END

109

Heather Tobis Booth represents several crucial connections: the civil rights movement, the movement against university complicity with the "War Machine," and the abortion rights movement within the emerging student radicalism.

THE HEATHER TOBIS BOOTH STORY

1964–66

STORY BY HEATHER
TOBIS BOOTH
& GENE BOOTH

ART BY GARY DUMM
FROM LAYOUTS
BY GENE BOOTH

DON'T USE MY GRADES TO MURDER STUDENTS

U. of Chicago Students Seize Building in Draft Protest
May 12, 1966

I JOINED THE **FRIENDS** OF **SNCC** AT THE UNIVERSITY OF **CHICAGO** IN **1964**.

PAUL BOOTH

ROBERT ROSS

RICHARD FLACKS

THAT **SAME** YEAR I MET **SDS** ORGANIZERS FOR THE **FIRST** TIME.

I WAS IN THE **MISSISSIPPI SUMMER** PROJECT AND MET **FANNIE LOU HAMER**.

LET WOMEN DECIDE

NO **MORE** PARIETALS

LET WOMEN DECIDE

I HELPED START A **WOMEN'S GROUP** THAT WAS, FOR **CHICAGO**, THE FORERUNNER OF THE **WOMEN'S LIBERATION** MOVEMENT. WE FOUGHT FOR AN END TO "PARIETALS," THE DISCRIMINATORY RULES FOR **WOMEN STUDENTS** THAT TREATED US LIKE CHILDREN.

IN DECEMBER 1965 SDS CONVENED A "RETHINKING" CONFERENCE FOR ITS MEMBERS IN DOWNSTATE, URBANA-CHAMPAIGN, UNIVERSITY OF ILLINOIS.

HERE, FOR THE **FIRST** TIME, A WORKSHOP OF **WOMEN ACTIVISTS** DECIDED TO BREAK OFF, TO HAVE A **MEETING** FOR **WOMEN ONLY.**

ARGUMENTS!

I'M **NOT** TRYING TO JOIN **THEIR GROUP**...WHAT'S YOUR PROBLEM?

SOMETHING NEW WAS STARTING IN **SDS**, TOO.

THAT SAME YEAR, **400** OF US GATHERED TO **PROTEST** AGAINST THE UNIVERSITY TURNING OVER **NAMES** OF **MALE** STUDENTS TO THEIR **DRAFT BOARDS**...

②

WE CAME INSIDE TO GET OUT OF THE RAIN...AND IT WAS A **SIT-IN!**

THE FIRST ONE SINCE THE **BERKELEY FREE SPEECH** MOVEMENT IN **1964.** AND IT WAS MY FUTURE HUSBAND, **PAUL BOOTH**, WHO CAME FROM THE **SDS** NATIONAL OFFICE TO **SPEAK** TO US.

A FORMER BOYFRIEND (HE WAS FUNNY, SWEET, PLAYED GUITAR, AND WAS FROM THE SOUTH) TOLD ME THAT HIS SISTER WAS PREGNANT...

AH'M FREAKIN' OUT!

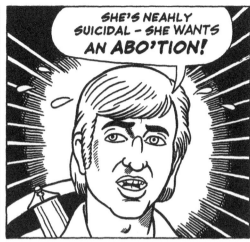

SHE'S NEAHLY SUICIDAL – SHE WANTS AN ABO'TION!

WE TALKED ABOUT THIS OUTSIDE IDA NOYES HALL AT THE UNIVERSITY OF CHICAGO.

WHAT'RE YOU GONNA DO?

SUCH ME... ENNY IDEAHS?

NOT REALLY. UMMM...

I REMEMBER NOT KNOWING WHAT TO DO, BUT THINKING "I'LL CALL DOCTORS FROM THE CIVIL RIGHTS MOVEMENT."

I WAS CONFUSED ABOUT WHAT TO ASK THE DOCTOR: WHAT WOULD HAPPEN? WAS IT DANGEROUS? WAS IT PAINFUL?...AND IF SO, WHEN? WHAT WAS THE FOLLOW-UP? HOW MUCH WOULD IT COST? WAS IT DANGEROUS FOR THE DOCTOR? HOW WOULD WE STAY IN CONTACT?

IN THOSE DAYS, TWO OR MORE PEOPLE DISCUSSING ABORTION COULD BE TREATED AS A CONSPIRACY TO COMMIT MURDER!

I KNEW HIS SISTER, BUT NEVER SPOKE TO HER DIRECTLY ABOUT THIS...MY CONTACT WAS WITH THE DOCTOR.

113

I CONTACTED SOMEONE AT THE **MEDICAL COMMITTEE FOR HUMAN RIGHTS** AND FOUND A DOCTOR WHO PERFORMED THE ABORTION **SUCCESSFULLY.** WORD GOT **AROUND** AND OTHERS **CALLED.**

PSST-PSST-PSST!

YOU DON'T SAY!

OVER THE NEXT FEW YEARS THIS BUILT TO BECOME **JANE,** ONE OF THE FIRST **ABORTION COUNSELING** SERVICES...

INFORMATION BROCHURE

What is Abortion Counseling Service?

We are women... ultimate goal... liberation...

THE LAW DIDN'T CHANGE UNTIL **JANUARY 22, 1973,** WITH THE **SUPREME COURT DECISION** IN **ROE V. WADE.**

KEEP ABORTION LEGAL

KEEP ABORTION LEGAL

KEEP ABORTION LEGAL

NOW

BY THE TIME THE LAW CHANGED, **JANE** ENDED UP ARRANGING OVER **11,000** ABORTIONS.

J/ANE

FYI: I RECENTLY LEARNED **MORE** ABOUT THE **FIRST** DOCTOR WHO WE **CONTACTED...** HE WAS AN EX-TRAORDINARILY **COURAGEOUS** AFRICAN AMERICAN FIGHTER FOR CIVIL **RIGHTS** FROM **MISSISSIPPI** AND ONLY **LEFT** WHEN HE FOUND HIS NAME ON A **KU KLUX KLAN DEATH** LIST BECAUSE OF HIS OUTSPOKEN **SUPPORT** FOR CIVIL RIGHTS.

HERE'S HOW I **LOOKED** IN '65: LONG BROWN HAIR, OFTEN IN A **PONYTAIL,** NAVY PULLOVER, DARK BLUE **DUNGAREES,** AND BLACK **BOOTS.**

The FUTURE

1965

-END-

AUSTIN STORIES
PART ONE

STORY BY MARIANN WIZARD WITH ALICE EMBREE AND HARVEY PEKAR
ART BY GARY DUMM

APRIL 1965 — ABOUT 40 PEOPLE, UNIVERSITY OF TEXAS MEMBERS OF SDS, ARE PROTESTING THE VIETNAM WAR IN FRONT OF PRESIDENT JOHNSON'S RANCH. THEY'RE BEING QUESTIONED BY REPORTERS.

STOP THE BOMBING

NEGOTIATE NOW

WE'RE HERE TO PETITION PRESIDENT JOHNSON...

NO WIDER WAR

PRESIDENT JOHNSON IS IN TEXAS FOR EASTER. THREE WEEKS EARLIER THE MISSION OF THE U.S. FORCES CHANGED FROM DEFENSIVE TO OFFENSIVE, THE FIRST STEP TO AMERICANIZATION OF THE GROUND WAR. AN SDS PROTEST TO WASHINGTON HAS DRAWN 25,000 PARTICIPANTS. OUTSIDE HIS GATES THE PICKETING AND QUESTIONING CONTINUE.

STOP THE BOMB!

WHAT DO YOU HOPE TO ACCOMPLISH BY BEING HERE?

END THE WAR NOW

END THE WAR!

A PRESIDENTIAL AIDE ACCEPTS A PETITION FROM THE PROTESTERS.

UNH...I'LL BE SURE THAT THE PRESIDENT GETS THIS.

OUT OF VIET-NA

WE'RE GONNA NEED A LOT MORE PEOPLE OUT HERE BEFORE THEY TAKE US SERIOUSLY.

115

THE CHUCK WAGON (THE STUDENT UNION EATERY AT UT) HOSTS AN **SDS** MEETING.

PRINT UP FLYERS!

WE'LL HAVE A **GOAT ROAST!**

AND SIGN UP **NEW** MEMBERS!

THEN SOME **FRAT BOYS** ENTER WITH **CAMERAS.**

WHAT ARE THE **FRAT BOYS** DOING IN HERE?

GOOD AFTERNOON, MY GOOD PEOPLE...I AM **ZARRYL FUNZUK**, HOLLYWOOD PRODUCER...I'M **FILMING** AN INTRAMURAL THRILLER, **"BOLDFINGER,"** WHICH WILL **PREMIERE** RIGHT HERE AT THE UNIVERSITY DURING **"ROUND-UP"** WEEK. ARE THERE, PERCHANCE, ANY **GENUINE BEATNIK CHICKS** HERE TODAY WHO **WISH** TO BECOME **MOVIE STARS?**

TWO FRESHMAN GIRLS **VOLUNTEER.**

HA! THEY WANT BEATNIK CHICKS...I'LL **SHOW** THEM A BEATNIK CHICK.

AT THE **SDS** TABLE...

WHOA! I KNOW THAT BLONDE, SHE'S FROM FT. WORTH, FROM MY HIGH SCHOOL.

THE OTHER ONE'S CALLED **"WEEZY,"** I THINK. SHE'S A **RICH** HIGH SCHOOL KID WHO **HANGS OUT** HERE AND IS **"EASY,"** THEY SAY.

BIRDS OF A FEATHER **FLOCK** TOGETHER.

WHY DO WOMEN **ACT** LIKE THAT?

WHY DO **MEN TALK** ABOUT 'EM LIKE THAT?

IN **MISSISSIPPI** WE SAW THAT PEOPLE SOMETIMES HAVE TO **DEPEND** ON **EACH OTHER** FOR THEIR LIVES, **MEN** AND **WOMEN**. SO WE **LEARNED** TO BE MORE **HONEST** ABOUT SAYING THAT CERTAIN BEHAVIOR IS **FOOLISH** OR **SELF-DESTRUCTIVE**, AND TO LISTEN IF OUR FRIENDS **CRITICIZED** OR MADE **SUGGESTIONS**. IF THOSE GIRLS WERE INVOLVED IN **THE MOVEMENT** THEY WOULDN'T HAVE **TIME** FOR FRATERNITY GAMES, AND YOU GUYS WOULDN'T SIT HERE AND **TALK** ABOUT THEM LIKE THAT EITHER!

117

STILL LATER AT A CIVIL RIGHTS DEMONSTRATION AT ROY'S LOUNGE, GEORGE V. IS ARRESTED.

ROY'S LOUNGE
CocaCola

ROY BYRD, CLEANERS TAILORS

THERE'S A GAP IN THE LINE... I'M STAYING!

HEY, GLAD YOU COULD MAKE IT! YOU MIGHT WANT TO TAKE OFF THOSE EARRINGS...THESE SORORITY GIRLS WILL RIP THEM OUT OF YOUR EAR LOBES.

BACK AT GEORGE'S APARTMENT...

LADIES, I'M PREPARED TO LOSE MY VIRGINITY TO EITHER ONE OF YOU, BUT NOT BOTH TOGETHER.

I'VE GOT CURFEW, AND VIRGINITY CAN TAKE A WHILE TO LOSE. I'LL SEE YOU LATER, GEORGE...HEY, LOUISE, DON'T HURT HIM TOO BAD!

SHE'S MY FRIEND... SHE KNEW I NEEDED SOMEONE TONIGHT.

BUT IT'S GEORGE AND MARIANN WHO LATER GET MARRIED...

119

IN 1965 THE VIETNAM WAR ESCALATES, THERE ARE **RIOTS** IN **WATTS**, WHITE SNCC MEMBERS ARE SENT HOME AND JOIN **ANTIWAR** AND **ANTIDRAFT** MOVEMENTS. THERE IS **RESISTANCE** TO SCHOOL ADMINISTRATIONS TRYING TO HOBBLE **SDS**...SO AT A BIG **TEXAS SDS** MEETING...

I WANT US TO **PUBLISH** AN **ALTERNATIVE WEEKLY** NEWSPAPER SO WE CAN **CONTROL** OUR **OWN** PUBLIC INFORMATION AND NOT **RELY** ON THE "DAILY TEXAN." WE COULD CALL IT "THE RAG."

SEVERAL OF US ARE PLANNING AN **ALL-WOMAN SIT-IN** AT STATE **SELECTIVE SERVICE** HEADQUARTERS. THE **DRAFT** AFFECTS **WOMEN**, TOO, EVEN THOUGH WE'RE NOT **SUBJECT** TO IT, AND WE WANT TO GET THAT **MESSAGE** OUT...THAT WOMEN HAVE A **STAKE** IN THIS ISSUE AND OUR **OPINION** COUNTS.

AT THE OPENING **SDS** MEETING THERE'S A **RECORD CROWD**...

SDS

I'D LIKE TO **WELCOME** ALL OF YOU TO THE FIRST **FALL MEETING** OF STUDENTS FOR A DEMOCRATIC SOCIETY...

IN OCTOBER 1966 "THE RAG" IS **FIRST** PRINTED.

AND AT THE STATE **SELECTIVE SERVICE** OFFICE TEN SDS WOMEN STAGE A **SIT-IN** PROTESTING THE DRAFT.

THE UNIVERSITY OF TEXAS WON'T ALLOW "THE RAG" TO BE SOLD ON CAMPUS...GEORGE IS ARRESTED FOR DOING SO.

GEORGE KEEPS ON SELLING THE PAPER, THOUGH.

YOU BETTER BELIEVE THE DRAFT AFFECTS ME; MY HUSBAND HAS TO TAKE A FULL LOAD OF CLASSES AND CAN'T WORK, SO I CAN'T TAKE CLASSES MYSELF.

WOMEN PROTEST DRAFT

DURING A PROTEST ON THE STATE CAPITOL STEPS, GEORGE RUSHES TO MARIANN'S AID.

IN 1967 SDS IS AT THE CENTER OF A MAJOR FREE SPEECH BATTLE.

A FREE UNIVERSITY IN A FREE SOCIETY

MILITAR OFF CAMPUS

VOTE SDS S

VOTE SDS SLATE

STUDENT BILL OF RIGHTS

150 DEMONSTRATORS WAIT TO PROTEST VICE PRESIDENT HUBERT HUMPHREY'S APPEARANCE AT THE TEXAS LEGISLATURE.

WON'T GO

OUT OF VIET-NAM

HUMPHREY NO

THE UNIVERSITY **REGENTS** RESPOND BY REVOKING **SDS'S** STATUS. GEORGE IS ARRESTED FOR USING **ABUSIVE LANGUAGE** AT A **HUMPHREY** DEMONSTRATION...

THIS IS THE **THIRD** TIME HE'S GONE TO **JAIL** THIS YEAR. I'M AFRAID HE'LL **LOSE** HIS JOB, AND WE CAN'T LIVE ON "**RAG**" SALES ALONE.

ON A SUNNY SUMMER DAY **GEORGE VIZARD** IS SHOT AND **KILLED** AT A **CONVENIENCE** STORE WHERE HE **WORKS**. IT WILL BE **FOURTEEN** YEARS BEFORE **ANYONE** IS HELD **ACCOUNTABLE** FOR THIS CRIME.

BLAM!

ASTROLOGY

AT AN **SDS** MEETING LATER...

WE DO NOT **KNOW** YET WHO HAS DONE **THIS** OR WHY...

...THEN IF THAT'S **HOW** THE **GAME** IS PLAYED, SO HELP ME I WILL **PLAY** MY HAND. THERE **WON'T** BE A **GAP** IN OUR LINES IF I CAN **HELP** IT. I DON'T **KNOW** IF I CAN **FILL** EVEN ONE OF HIS SHOES, BUT I'LL **TRY**, IF YOU'LL HELP ME **WALK** IN THEM.

END

Vignettes from NEW ORLEANS

STORY BY
ERIC GORDON &
HARVEY PEKAR
ART BY
GARY DUMM

ERIC GORDON

IN AUGUST 1966 I'M OFF TO GRADUATE SCHOOL, **TULANE UNIVERSITY** IN **NEW ORLEANS**. TULANE HAD JUST **INTEGRATED** A COUPLE OF YEARS BEFORE, SO I DON'T THINK THEY WERE QUITE **USED TO** PEOPLE LIKE ME, WHO WOULD **SOONER** TALK ABOUT **IMPERIALISM** THAN ABOUT BEER, DATING, AND DOPE.

GET OUT NOW!

I ORGANIZED THE TULANE CHAPTER OF SDS AND WE WERE GOING STRONG FOR A COUPLE OF YEARS. I WAS SO PROUD WHEN THE SENATE **INTELLIGENCE COMMITTEE** NAMED TULANE AS ONE OF THE **TOP TEN** CAMPUSES IN THE COUNTRY, ALONGSIDE **COLUMBIA, MICHIGAN, WISCONSIN, AND BERKELEY,** THAT WERE READY TO **EXPLODE** IN OPEN REVOLUTION.

MY PHOTO SHOWED UP IN SOME **FANTASY SDS** PYRAMID OF POWER THAT THE **SENATE** GENERATED, BUT IT DIDN'T LOOK LIKE ANY FLOW CHART I WAS **EVER** AWARE OF. SOMETHING TO WRITE HOME ABOUT. I WOULD **LATER** LEARN THROUGH THE **FREEDOM OF INFORMATION ACT** THAT MY MAIL WAS **REGULARLY INTERCEPTED** AND READ.

A COUPLE BECAME ACTIVE WITH OUR **NEW ORLEANS** SDS MOVEMENT, **GIL** AND **JILL SCHAFER. JILL** GOT ONTO A WOMEN'S TRIP TO **COMMUNIST CHINA** – THIS WAS AT A TIME WHEN PRACTICALLY SPEAKING **ONLY** REVOLUTIONARIES TRAVELED THERE – AND CAME BACK WITH **GLOWING** REPORTS OF COMMUNES AND BAREFOOT DOCTORS AND **CHAIRMAN MAO.**

I CAN'T SAY **ENOUGH** ABOUT **CHAIRMAN MAO.**

GIL WAS A BIT OF A **LOOSE CANNON...**

MORE THAN **ONCE** HE PROPOSED SOME **HEAVY-DUTY ACTION,** LIKE **BREAKING** STORE WINDOWS, THAT NO ONE ELSE SEEMED **PRE-PARED** TO DO. BUT ONE THING HE SUGGESTED, IN 1968, DID KIND OF **EXCITE** OUR FANCY.

DOWN IN THE **FRENCH QUARTER,** THE **OWNERS OF JAZZ** CLUBS, LIKE **AL HIRT** AND **PETE FOUNTAIN,** WERE PUTTING IT TO POLICE THAT THE **OPEN PRESENCE** AND VISIBILITY OF HOMOSEXUALS AND CROSS-DRESSERS WAS INTERFERING WITH **TOURIST BUSINESS.** MIND YOU, THIS IS **NEW ORLEANS,** HOME OF THE **MARDI GRAS,** THE **CITY THAT CARE FORGOT.**

YOU KNOW "LAISSEZ LES BON TEMPS ROULEZ," RIGHT? SO THE POLICE HAD ACTUALLY STARTED ARRESTING WOMEN ON BOURBON STREET WHO WERE WEARING JEANS! GIL FIGURED IT WOULD BE A GOOD MOVE FOR SDS TO SHOW SOME SOLIDARITY, AND SO WE TOOK OURSELVES DOWN TO THE FRENCH QUARTER AND JOINED THE PROTESTS. THIS WAS ABOUT A YEAR BEFORE STONEWALL. THE POLICE EASED UP. (NOT TOO LONG AFTER, WE LEARNED THAT GIL AND JILL HAD BEEN LONGTIME FBI AGENTS.)

STUDENTS FOR A DEMOCRATIC SOCIETY WAS THE STUDENT ORGANIZATION, AND I WAS SOMETHING OF A PUBLIC BÊTE NOIR AROUND NEW ORLEANS. I'D BEEN ARRESTED A FEW TIMES FOR ANTIWAR ACTIVITY, MARCHED IN DOZENS OF DEMONSTRATIONS, HANDED OUT THOUSANDS OF LEAFLETS, COUNSELED YOUNG MEN ON THEIR ALTERNATIVES TO SERVING IN THE MILITARY. GOVERNMENT OPERATIVES FOLLOWED ME, TAPPED MY PHONE, AND, I HAVE REASON TO BELIEVE, BROKE INTO MY APARTMENT ONCE.

I LIVED UPSTAIRS FROM A LAUNDRY. I TRIED TO REMAIN RELATIVELY ANONYMOUS ON MY BLOCK AND STAYED PARTICULARLY CLEAR OF MY IMMEDIATE NEIGHBORS, A FAMILY INELEGANTLY BUT BEST DESCRIBED AS POOR WHITE TRASH. THERE WAS A SULLEN WIFE SURROUNDED BY THREE OR FOUR BAREFOOT BRATS...

...AND A LOUD, HARD-DRINKING MAN WHOSE MEANS OF SUPPORT WERE INVISIBLE TO MY EYES. DECALS PASTED ON THE FRONT DOOR GLASS SEEMED TO SAY IT ALL: THE PLAYBOY BUNNY AND A CONFEDERATE FLAG.

ONE DAY IN LATE SPRING OR SUMMER I RETURNED HOME AROUND 7 P.M. MY NEIGHBOR EMERGED FROM HIS SHOTGUN BUNGALOW AND APPROACHED.

COUPLE GUYS AROUND HERE LOOKING FOR YOU TODAY.

OH?

YEP. DROVE UP TOGETHER. ONE STAYED IN THE CAR, THE OTHER WENT UP TO ALL THE NEIGHBORS ASKING QUESTIONS.

HUH, WONDER WHAT THAT'S ABOUT?

LISSEN, BUDDY, I SEEN HOW THEM BOYS OPERATE. FED'RAL AGENTS, YA KNOW.

LOOK, AH DON'T KNOW WHUT YER DOIN' OR ANYTHIN', BUT DON'T WORRY...I DIDN' TELL THEM NUTHIN'. YER SAFE WITH ME...AH'M IN TH' KLAN.

END

124

Almost every male SDSer,
like hundreds of thousands
of other college students,
faced the prospect of the
draft from 1965 onward.

MY LIFE AT STAKE

STORY BY **PAUL BUHLE**
ART BY **GARY DUMM**

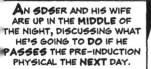

AN SDSER AND HIS WIFE ARE UP IN THE MIDDLE OF THE NIGHT, DISCUSSING WHAT HE'S GOING TO DO IF HE PASSES THE PRE-INDUCTION PHYSICAL THE NEXT DAY.

WHERE **DID** THOSE **TWO** WEEKS GO?!

THE **PEACE MARCH** SEEMS LIKE A **MILLION** YEARS AGO!

REPORT FOR PRE-INDUCTION PHYSICAL

GREETINGS,

I **DON'T** WANT TO MOVE TO **CANADA**. I DON'T WANT **YOU** TO GO TO JAIL. I DON'T KNOW **WHICH** I DON'T WANT **MORE**.

AND I **DON'T** WANT THEM TO **PUSH** ME OUT OF **MY** COUNTRY. BUT MAYBE IT'S **NOT** MY COUNTRY ANY-MORE.

THEY SLEEP NERVOUSLY...

AND AWAKEN **LATER** THAT NIGHT.

WHAT WOULD **JAIL** BE LIKE? MAYBE **CANADA** WOULD BE BETTER. WE COULD **GO** TO **SCHOOL** UP THERE, TOO.

IF THAT'S **WHAT** YOU WANT.

THEY SLEEP **AGAIN**, FITFULLY. AND MORNING, WITHOUT **MUCH** PROMISE, FINALLY ARRIVES.

WELL, WHAT DID **WE DECIDE?**

NO. I **MADE** UP MY MIND. I'M GOING TO **JAIL**.

127

GETTING ON THE BUS...

PLEASE LOOK AT THIS, ONE SIDE IS IN **SPANISH.**

ON THE WAY TO THE INDUCTION CENTER...

I GUESS WE **ALL** HAVE SOMETHING TO **READ** ON THE TRIP.

IN LINE AT THE **DRAFT BOARD** HE PULLS OUT A HANDMADE **SIGN**...

PHYSICAL EXAM

DON'T GO I'M NOT GOING

PUT **THAT** AWAY! YOU'LL GET INTO **TROUBLE!**

BROTHERS, **DON'T** SIGN ANY-THING. **DON'T** SIGN AWAY YOUR LIVES!

DON'T GO I'M NOT GOING

ARE **YOU** GONNA MAKE **TROUBLE???**

THE SDSER PUTS THE SIGN **AWAY** AS HE'S TAKEN ASIDE.

MADISON STRIKE

STORY BY
PAUL BUHLE
ART BY
GARY DUMM

THE STATUE OF ABRAHAM LINCOLN SITS IMPASSIVELY THROUGH THE **ALMOST** FESTIVE ATMOSPHERE AS STILT-WALKERS, STUDENTS, THE **SAN FRANCISCO MIME TROUPE,** AND **MISS SIFTING AND WINNOWING (VICKI GABRINER)** DO THEIR THING.

BUT ALL TOO SOON THE AIR WILL BE **FILLED** WITH TEAR GAS AND THE **SMELL** OF BLOOD AND CRIES OF ANGER AND FEAR.

131

IN HIS OFFICE DEAN JOSEPH KAUFFMAN RECALLS HIS ADMIRATION FOR JFK BUT STILL INSISTS...

THE STUDENTS HAVE GONE TOO FAR... WE HAVE TO LET THE COPS GO IN!

STUDENT LEADERS **OFFER** TO ASSIST THE POLICE IN **ESCORTING** THE **DOW** RECRUITERS **OFF** CAMPUS ON THE CONDITION THAT THEY WILL **NOT** RETURN.

THE LEADERS ASK THE CROWD: WOULD THE SIT-IN **END** ON THAT CONDITION? THE **ANSWER** IS...

YES!

A JUDGE IS CONSULTED ABOUT THE **CONFRONTATION**...

NO, THERE IS NO EVIDENCE THAT POLICE WILL BE EXCESSIVELY BRUTAL.

AND **SUDDENLY** POLICE ARE ON THE OTHER SIDE OF THE GLASS DOORS, WITH **CLUBS** LIFTED UP, READY TO STRIKE.

THEY AT-TEMPT TO **PUSH** IN, AND THE **CROWD, PACKED** AGAINST THE DOORS, **PUSHES** BACK.

135

OTHERS LIKE **CHUCK SCHWARTZ** AREN'T SO **LUCKY:** IN THE FRONT LINE, HE IS **BASHED** ON THE **HEAD** AND **BLOODIED** UNDER **TWO** COPS WITH BATONS...

...WHEN HALF A DOZEN DEMONSTRATORS **JUMP** ON **TOP** OF THEM, AND HE **SQUEEZES** OUT **UNDERNEATH.**

SCHWARTZ RETURNS TO RAGING AT THE POLICE BEFORE GOING TO GET STITCHES...

THE SAN FRANCISCO MIME TROUPE, ON THE SCENE ALL DAY, STAGES A PANTOMIME ACTION IN FRONT OF THE CROWD...

THE POLICE REGAIN THEIR COMPOSURE...

THUP!

...AND THE FIRST TEAR GAS CANNISTER IS LOBBED INTO THE CROWD.

BUT THE STUDENTS KNOW WHAT TO DO NOW.

THEY WRAP IT AND THROW IT RIGHT BACK.

VIOLENCE BEGINS AGAIN WITH ANOTHER TEAR GAS CANNISTER BARRAGE TO BEGIN BREAKING UP THE DEFIANT CROWD.

THWP!

TUMP! THUP! TUP!

AND THEN THE POLICE WADE IN WITH THEIR CLUBS...

DETERMINED TO DRIVE THE COUGHING CROWD FROM THE EXTENDED HILL.

GASP! KOFF! KOFF!

THAT EVENING AT THE MEMORIAL UNION THEATER. GEORGE MOSSE RISES TO INSIST...

...THE UNIVERSITY HAS OVERREACTED.

I AGREE, AND I'D LIKE TO PROPOSE A RESOLUTION CONDEMNING "INDISCRIMINATE VIOLENCE" BY THE POLICE.

BUT THE POLICE HAVE BEEN THREATENED BY THE STUDENT BRUTALITY!

THE CHANCELLOR CHALLENGES THE FACULTY...

YOU HAVEN'T THE GUTS TO SUPPORT ME!

...AND HIS EMOTIONAL APPEAL WORKS! THE VOTE GOES IN HIS FAVOR, AGAINST CONDEMNING HIS ADMINISTRATION'S ACTIONS...THE FACULTY THEN FILES OUT INTO THE DARKENED STREET.

STRIKE STRIKE STRIKE

IT'S GETTING COLD, BUT WE CAN SING TO KEEP WARM...

...I KNOW THE WORDS UPDATING AN OLD UNION SONG...

...AND I'LL TEACH IT TO EVERYONE WHO WANTS TO LEARN. IT STARTS, "WHICH SIDE ARE YOU ON..."

143

145

THE STUDENT **STRIKE** PETERED OUT AFTER A GLORIOUS **TEN DAYS. SDS** ITSELF DID NOT ACTUALLY GET MUCH **LARGER** IN MEMBERSHIP. BUT WE WERE **WRONG** TO BE PESSIMISTIC. WE PLAYED OUR ROLE **EFFECTIVELY** BY SELLING "**CONNECTIONS,**" SPEAKING IN THE STUDENT DORMS, AND WORKING WITHIN A WIDE RANGE OF ORGANIZATIONS THAT SPOKE **AGAINST** THE **WAR** AND FOR **STUDENT** POWER. MOST **IMPORTANT**, DESPITE THE BLOODY REALITY OF POLICE VIOLENCE, THE STUDENTS **GAINED** SELF-CONFIDENCE IN THEIR **OWN POLITICAL** ABILITIES.

REMEMBERING 1968

STORY BY
FREDY PERLMAN & PAUL BUHLE

ART BY
GARY DUMM

The starting point of my conscious life the way that I think about it now—was the one time when I was engaged in a group project.

No outside force, no institution, no boss or leader defined our project, made our decisions, determined our schedules or tasks. We briefly succeeded in creating a real community, a condition that doesn't exist in today's societies, whatever the system is called, and therefore isn't even understood.

If I hadn't, once in my life, collaborated with people who stopped being "students" or "teachers" or "wage workers" and became something else for a little while, I might never have thought about any other possibility. But it did happen. If I hadn't once earlier experienced friendship, solidarity, and communications like this...but I did.

147

Some people think that the foremen and the liberal university administrators that we have now have proved that we won something. Not me: they won in spite of us, not because of us. I don't see people engaged in projects chosen by they themselves, without supervisors or guards.

AMERICA 1960

I WAS AN IMMIGRANT FROM LATIN AMERICA, WITH **PARENTS** ESCAPING NAZISM, AND THEN ESCAPING THIRD-WORLD **POVERTY**. THE WORLD TO WHICH I WAS BROUGHT WAS PUBLICLY CONSIDERED HUMANITY'S FIRST EARTHLY **PARADISE**, THE MOST **PERFECT** COMMUNITY OF HAPPY HUMAN BEINGS. BY 1960, IN AMERICA, I WAS SEEING SOMETHING **DIFFERENT**.

148

SLOWLY, I BEGAN TO REALIZE THAT AMERICA WAS A LAND OF GIGANTIC TOYS THAT HAVE OVERWHELMED THE PEOPLE. AS I BEGAN TO SEE IT, OBJECTS RULED CITY STREETS, COUNTRY HIGHWAYS, BRIDGES, AND UNDERPASSES.

BIG STORE

OBJECTS WERE HOUSED, FED, AND NURSED; OBJECTS WERE DISPLAYED, PRAISED, HONORED, AND WORSHIPPED.

BUY

THE PEOPLE I MET WERE SMALL AND FEARFUL.

WHEN THEY WERE NOT NURSING THE OBJECTS, THEY LOOKED LIKE NOTHING MORE THAN OBSTACLES IN THE PATHS OF RUSHING OBJECTS AND VEHICLES.

NEARLY EVERY COLLISION BETWEEN A PERSON AND AN OBJECT DESTROYED THE PERSON WHILE LEAVING THE OBJECT INTACT.

149

BY 1968 I WAS BACK FROM PARIS, WHERE I SAW AND TOOK PART IN THE MAY 1968 STUDENT AND WORKER REVOLT THAT ALMOST OVERTHREW PRESIDENT De GAULLE AND THE WHOLE CAPITALIST SYSTEM THERE.

BE REALISTIC... DEMAND THE IMPOSSIBLE

MY NEW WORLD WAS KALAMAZOO, MICHIGAN, WHERE I TAUGHT AND HELPED BRING TOGETHER A GROUP TO PUBLISH A NEW KIND OF MAGAZINE, "BLACK AND RED." IT WAS INSPIRED BY THE WORKER-STUDENT REVOLT IN PARIS. BUT IT WAS BASED ON OUR EXPERIENCE IN A TYPICAL AMERICAN UNIVERSITY, TOO.

COVER TO FREDY'S BOOK WRITTEN IN 1969...

THE REPRODUCTION OF DAILY LIFE

"BLACK AND RED" ENDED SOON AFTER FREDY PERLMAN LEFT SDS AND MOVED TO DETROIT, WHERE AN ANARCHIST PRESS WAS ESTABLISHED. IT PRINTED THE SDS MAGAZINE "RADICAL AMERICA," AND IT LASTED FOR MORE THAN A DECADE.

DETROIT PRINT CO-OP

END

$\mathcal{S}$DS was rocking the nation's campuses, but in New York the "Old Left" still predominated. And building mass demonstrations against the war, I quickly learned, meant balancing the views of an unruly bunch of political organizations and tendencies—

From liberals and social democrats . . .

How about this idea for the demo logo?

I don't know . . . couldn't you make it more polite?

We have Communists in the coalition?!

to Trotskyists and Communists . . .

Way too multi-issue! [If you want multi-issue join us!]

"Stop the War"? That's it? Too damned single-issue!

to pacifists and resisters . . .

I'm not seeing any civil disobedience there!

Moral suasion forever!

not to mention the many groups that didn't carry as much weight in the coalition— or didn't really want to be part of it.

Bourgeois!

Sell-out!

I'm outta here!

It was enough to give a young agit-artist nightmares—*until* . . .

No! No more logos!

At last— something for everyone!

P.S. A variation —*sans* beret and gun—finally saw the light of day in 1970. (But I lost that button a long time ago.)

April 1968 saw hundreds of thousands of demonstrators fill Central Park's Sheep Meadow and the Columbia University student strike. But by June frustration over the escalating war and the old tactic of building seasonal, single-issue mass mobilizations split the Student Mobilization Committee—

TO BE OR NOT TO BE? SMC

CONTINUATIONS June 29&2 NEW YORK CITY COMMITTEE

152

SANE–Committee for a Sane Nuclear Policy; *WSP*–Women Strike for Peace; *YSA*–Young Socialist Alliance; *DuBois*–DuBois Club; *WRL*– War Resisters League; *Resistance*; *YAWF*–Youth Against War and Fascism; *Yippies*; *SNCC*–Student Nonviolent Coordinating Committee.

*O*ut of which hatched a new organization: the *Radical Organizing Committee.*

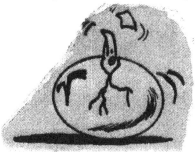

[Remnant of a ROC leaflet.]

A multi-issue organization directed toward liberal college students not yet ready for the radical plunge to SDS. A sort of radical halfway house . . .

Or, to use the parlance of the contemporary Establishment, if SDS was the hard stuff, ROC would be the entry drug.

For a few brief, heady months in the spring and summer of 1968, ROC got down to work. SDS, in New York City, was less than enthusiastic, but a lot of goodwill came our way, including office space at the Greenwich Village Peace Center.

Legitimacy is a warm desk— and telephone.

Then there was the ROC publicity jugger-naut: ads, leaflets, stickers—even a mascot (courtesy of the *Arabian Nights* [see above]). And, for me, an *almost* elegant logo . . .

Well, okay, obscure is more like it (the radical sign courtesy of a comrade major-ing in chemistry).

Except for the Yippies, ROC was the New Left media success of the year!

And soon we had a focus – one first raised in a mysterious May meeting called by the National Mobilization Committee's Tom Hayden, held in a sparsely furnished Upper West Side apartment.

We'll surround the Democratic Convention, stop Humphrey, demand the platform and the war . . .

And what? Nominate RFK?

Dunno what you're talking about.

Whatever Hayden's plans were, by July Bobby Kennedy had been assassinated and the mobilization was headed for Chicago, with ROC in tow.

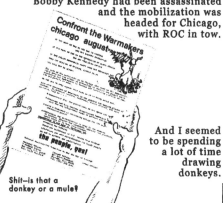

Confront the Warmakers chicago august

the people, yes!

Shit—is that a donkey or a mule?

And I seemed to be spending a lot of time drawing donkeys.

153

August 22: I arrived in the blistering hot city and joined the protest preparations.

This is how Tokyo students do the snake dance. Once all the protesters arrive, we control the streets!

At national mobilization planning meetings ROC established itself as a creative, if not particularly enlightened, force . . . .

OK—Women Strike for Peace'll picket the Hilton; the Friends'll march on the Amphitheater...

Nobody's talked to the National Guard sent here. We're doing that.

Fucking A!

Right on!

What exactly're you gonna do?

Oh, the girls in ROC will go to where some of 'em are posted and leaflet.

The Yippies'll do the Pigasus thing at the Civic Center; LBJ's Un-Birthday Party is at the Coliseum; SDS is recruiting McCarthy kids. What about ROC?

. . . and briefly won SDS's endorsement.

Fuck these other guys—SDS 'n ROC will take care of business!

The ROC action, such as it was, went off without a hitch. And it's safe to say that, until now, it was lost to history (as is the leaflet I made for the occasion).

154

*R*OC helped run the New York Movement Center in Hyde Park and coordinate the activities of NYC groups. But what raised the ire of the Chicago Police was . . .

. . . OUR FLAG!

(This faded photo is the last shred of evidence.)

A concoction of felt, cheap silk, and Elmer's Glue, it announced ROC's presence at the August 28 Grant Park rally—

and, as it turned out, it also came in handy as a way to locate your buddies after a police charge...

...when not provoking one (i.e., police charge) on its own.

We heard over the police band the pigs're gonna bust everyone around the flag!

Fall 1968 was anticlimactic, as boycotts tend to be.

(It took a while before I got Nixon right.)

As was ROC's final action.

But 1969 beckoned . . .

BLACK PANTHERS ANTI-FASCISM CONFERENCE OAKLAND . . .

Josh, you better stop drawing.

The Panthers think you're a cop.

END

155

JBROWN 2006

The SDS magazine's residential home base until late 1971 was a two-family house in a blue-collar neighborhood. Months after the departure of the magazine's editor, it was raided by the local FBI, which hauled away all the uncollated pages of back issues.

Story by Paul Buhle
Art by Gary Dumm

1968

THE SDS MAGAZINE

FILLMORE

MORE **MAGAZINES** TO **SEND**, FRED.

U.S. POST OFFICE

IT **WASN'T** A ONE-PERSON MAGAZINE, NOT **REALLY**. I HAD **LOTS** OF HELP. BUT THE **ONLY** MAGAZINE PUBLISHED FOR **SDS** FOR MORE THAN A FEW ISSUES WAS **THIS ONE**, AND IT CAME OUT TO **SEVERAL THOUSAND** MEMBERS, **SIX TIMES A YEAR!**

IT WAS **PRETTY POPULAR** WITH **GRADUATE** STUDENTS LIKE **MYSELF**, AND TOO **UNPOPULAR** WITH UNDERGRADUATE **SDSERS**, WHO **DIDN'T** READ ALL THAT MUCH. BUT **WE TRIED**.

HOLD ON, I THINK I'VE GOT IT...

...AN SDS COMIC BOOK WITH WONDER WART-HOG!...

...AND A WHOLE GANG OF IDIOTS. THIS WILL GET THE MESSAGE OUT THERE!

COME TO BED, PAUL...

Next day composing a letter to Gilbert Shelton, creator of Wonder Warthog...

GILBERT! I'VE BEEN SELLING "FEDS AND HEADS" AT THE SDS TABLE. AND A FOUNDATION JUST GAVE ME $2,000. ENOUGH FOR YOU TO DO THE COMIC!

And so, in San Francisco, Gilbert Shelton begins working...

159

C.L.R.! WE ARE PUBLISHING AN **ANTHOLOGY** OF YOUR WRITINGS IN "*RADICAL AMERICA*." THE FIRST ANTHOLOGY **ANYWHERE**...FOR SDSERS AND OTHERS.

BUTTER? COFFEE?

ONLY MARMALADE. AND TEA.

SO BRITISH!

THAT WAS LIFE IN **COLONIAL TRINIDAD.** WE ALSO LEARNED **SHAKESPEARE,** YOU KNOW. AND **CRICKET.** THAT WAS **MY LIFE,** CRICKET. SUCH A **DISAPPOINTMENT** TO MY PARENTS, THEY **WANTED** ME TO BE A **LAWYER** OR A **POLITICIAN.**

YOU CHOSE **SPORTS.**

AND THAT'S HOW I DECIDED TO **BECOME A REVOLUTIONARY.** THE WHITES WERE **NO BETTER** THAN **US.** I LEARNED **THAT** ON THE CRICKET **PITCH.**

AND YOU BECAME A **WRITER** THERE?

NOT REALLY. I **WROTE** A COUPLE OF PIECES ON HOW **CARIBBEAN BLACKS** HAD TO BE ON THE **TEST** TEAM, THE TEAM FOR THE **WORLD CUP.** BUT I BECAME A WRITER IN A **DIFFERENT** WAY. I WAS A SCHOOLTEACHER. AND I USED TO GO OVER AND TALK TO THE **WOMEN** IN THE BARRACKS, YOU KNOW, THE **KEPT** WOMEN. I TALKED TO THEM, THAT'S **ALL.** THEY **LIKED** A YOUNG MAN, MIDDLE CLASS AND PROPER, COMING **OVER** TO SEE THEM. I ASKED ABOUT THEIR **LIVES** AND THEY **TOLD** ME, LEAVING OUT **NOTHING.** IT WAS QUITE A **THING.**

LIKE ME **NOW,** YOU PUBLISHED A **MAGAZINE?**

OH, YES. IT **SHOCKED** THE LITERARY CLASS OF THE ISLAND. AND THEY **WANTED** TO BE **SHOCKED.**

THEY **STAYED** AND YOU LEFT...

THEY WERE **BROWN.** I WAS **BLACK.**

...BUT **YOU** CAME BACK A **REVOLUTIONARY.**

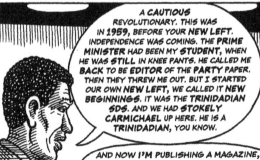

A **CAUTIOUS** REVOLUTIONARY. THIS WAS IN 1959, BEFORE YOUR **NEW LEFT.** INDEPENDENCE WAS COMING. THE **PRIME MINISTER** HAD BEEN MY **STUDENT,** WHEN HE WAS **STILL** IN KNEE PANTS. HE CALLED ME **BACK** TO BE **EDITOR** OF THE **PARTY PAPER.** THEN THEY THREW ME OUT. BUT I STARTED OUR OWN **NEW LEFT,** WE CALLED IT **NEW BEGINNINGS.** IT WAS THE **TRINIDADIAN SDS.** AND WE HAD **STOKELY CARMICHAEL** UP HERE. HE IS A **TRINIDADIAN,** YOU KNOW.

AND NOW I'M PUBLISHING A MAGAZINE, FOR SDS. THE ISSUE OF **YOUR** WRITINGS WILL BE THE **BIGGEST** WE'VE EVER PUBLISHED. AND WILL REACH **MORE** PEOPLE.

MAKE **SURE** THEY GET IT IN **ALL** THE PLACES WHERE THEY **KNOW** ME...IN **BRIXTON,** THAT **LONDON** NEIGHBORHOOD, IN **DETROIT,** IN **TORONTO** AND **MONTREAL** AND **JAMAICA** AND IN **ANTIGUA,** TOO.

WE'LL GET THEM **AROUND.** ONE **DOLLAR** A COPY! SIXTY CENTS FOR FIVE OR MORE!

IOWA
SDS
STORY

by David Rosheim and Harvey Pekar

Art by Gary Dumm

KROPOTKIN

GOLDMAN

It was not altogether clear to me what I was getting into. I should by rights have been starting my work as a **CONSCIENTIOUS OBJECTOR**, but the sight of the **CHICAGO** police assaulting my peers in **GRANT PARK** in **AUGUST 1968** disoriented me so badly that I went down to **IOWA CITY** in the fall of that **ANNUS MIRABILIS** to try to stir up the university students to help bring about the kind of ideal society I had envisioned.

I wanted the success of what I call "**ANARCHO SURREALISM.**" This meant, putting it very briefly, the unfettering of human thought and creativity and a blossoming of strange new kinds of beauty in the framework of a decentralized, humanistic, socialistic order. My definition of **ANARCHISM** does not differ from that of **PRINCE KROPOTKIN** or **EMMA GOLDMAN**; only my emphasis on the role of the imagination was new.

Very many students at the University of **IOWA** were enraged at the behavior of **DALEY'S** police and flocked to the initial meeting of the local **SDS**, of which I was a card-carrying member. I sat with them and watched how their desire for concrete action was muted by the peculiar, obscurationist tactics of the **SDS OFFICERS**, who were almost entirely members of the **PROGRESSIVE LABOR PARTY** (PLP, a.k.a. PL, A MAOIST organization in those days, but not so new ever since RICHARD M. NIXON shook hands with the late chairman).

The previous **JUNE** I had attended the SDS convention in **EAST LANSING, MICHIGAN**, where the great rift in the organization had become apparent. One now had to **SPECIFY** what kind of radical he was. I thought my sentiments lay with the anarchists, and I embraced the black banner to the immense disgust of the other **IOWA CITY** delegates, who were supporters of the **MAOIST PLP**. The lines had been drawn for the fall, and the strange campaign for the hearts of the rebellious students was all set to begin.

It was obvious to me that the **MARXIST** adherents of PL were very skilled politically. With some of them I had attended the previous **MAY** a student-labor symposium in **CHICAGO,**

PL

LENIN

MAO

ANTIWAR

SDS

I.W.W.

David Roshe

FANON

BAKUNIN

HSP

WHERE A YOUNG MAN BY THE NAME OF **EARL SILBAR** HAD GIVEN US AN ORGANIZATIONAL LECTURE. THE **PLERS** ALSO HAD REGULAR EVENING MEETINGS TO STUDY THE WORKS OF **LENIN** AND **MAO**. THEY ALSO ACHIEVED A **CONSENSUS** ON WHAT TOPICS WOULD BE ENCOURAGED DURING THE **MONDAY** NIGHT **SDS** MEETINGS IN THE **IOWA MEMORIAL UNION**. **CARMEN KRAMER** AND BRUCE CLARK WERE THE STRONGEST SUPPORTERS OF PL ON CAMPUS, AND MS. **KRAMER** SERVED AS THE HEAD OF THE **UNIVERSITY OF IOWA SDS**.

I WATCHED WITH ANNOYANCE AS THE TURNOUT FOR THE **SDS** MEETINGS DWINDLED AWAY DUE TO THE DELIBERATE, DULL PROCRASTINATION OF THE **PL FACTION**. NO ACTIONS WERE PLANNED, **NOTHING** HAPPENED. THE REASON FOR THIS **PL TACTIC** WAS THAT THEY WOULD BE OUTVOTED BY ACTIVIST **NON-PLERS** IF THE SIZE OF THE LOCAL **SDS** WERE TO INCREASE BY VERY MANY. FOR MY PART, I ASKED AROUND AND FOUND A CERTAIN **JERRY SIES** WAS THE LOCAL ANARCHIST IN RESIDENCE. I MET WITH HIM IN THE **GOLDEN FEATHER ROOM** OF THE **MEMORIAL UNION** AND TOLD HIM MY IDEAS. I WANTED TO PROPAGANDIZE FOR REVOLUTIONARY SURREALISM AND ANARCHISM, BUT TO DO SO FAIRLY COVERTLY, **"THE REVOLUTION BY NIGHT,"** AND TO TRY TO ORGANIZE AN ANARCHIST FACTION IN **SDS** TO PROMOTE MORE CAMPUS ANTIWAR AND ANTICORPORATE ACTIVITIES. HE **AGREED** TO THIS. IT HAD BEEN ONE OF HIS PROJECTS, TOO. I CONVINCED HIM OF MY SYNDICALIST SYMPATHIES BY SHOWING HIM MY **IWW** MEMBERSHIP CARD, WHICH I HAD GOTTEN IN **JULY**.

RADICAL ACTIVITY WAS AT A STANDSTILL DURING THE FIRST TWO WEEKS OF **SEPTEMBER**. WE ATTEMPTED TO ORGANIZE AN **SDS RALLY** IN FRONT OF THE HISTORIC OLD CAPITOL, A SPLENDID STRUCTURE THEN USED FOR THE OFFICES OF GRADUATE STUDIES AND THE UNIVERSITY ADMINISTRATORS. THE **PROGRESSIVE LABOR** PEOPLE WERE NOT CONVINCED AND ALL THAT WAS ACCOMPLISHED WAS THE PREPARATION OF A RADICAL READING LIST: **MARCUSE, MAO, FANON, BAKUNIN** (I HAD INSERTED SOME ANARCHIST AUTHORS), AND SO ON. FINALLY IT OCCURRED TO US TO ADAPT THE **HAWKEYE STUDENT PARTY (HSP)** TO THE CURRENT CAMPUS CIRCUMSTANCES. THE PARTY HAD BEGUN AS A LIBERAL-PACIFIST ORGANIZATION THAT HAD TRIED, AND FAILED, THE PREVIOUS SCHOOL YEAR TO ELECT ANTI-WAR **KEN WESSELS**, STUDENT BODY PRESIDENT, INSTEAD OF THE USUAL YOUNG **REPUBLICAN** FRATERNITY MEMBER. THE HSP WAS STILL ON THE ROLLS AS A VALID CAMPUS ORGANIZATION WITH THE RIGHT TO USE THE UNION FOR MEETINGS. THE WORD WAS SPREAD TO THE STUDENT AND NONSTUDENT ANARCHISTS, SURREALISTS, AND OTHER LIBERTARIAN SOCIALISTS TO ATTEND THE **FIRST** MEETING OF THE REVISED **HSP**.

APPROXIMATELY **FIFTEEN** PEOPLE APPEARED, **KEN WESSELS** AMONG THEM, AND I WAS PLEASED TO MAKE NEW FRIENDS. THERE WAS **BOB ECKHART**, A BLOND MUSTACHED FELLOW WHO HAD JUST RETURNED FROM **VIETNAM**, WHERE HE HAD SERVED WITH THE ARMY K-9 CORPS; **PAT KEARNEY**, A PART-TIME WORKER AT THE UNIVERSITY; **"TALL" PAT**, WHOSE LAST NAME I HAVE LOST, WHO WAS A FRESHMAN, AND ECKHART'S GIRLFRIEND; **PAUL McKIBBEN**, A COLLEGE DROPOUT FROM **MISSOURI** WHO WAS SLOWLY DRIFTING NORTHWARD INTO **CANADA**, BUT WHO PAUSED IN **IOWA CITY** LONG ENOUGH FOR US TO SHARE HIS INTENSE CONFUSION; **MARY MATKOV**, A QUIET UNDERCLASSMAN WHO DID NOT AT ALL RESEMBLE THE POPULAR IMAGE OF A **RADICAL** STUDENT. THERE WERE SEVERAL OTHERS, TOO, WHO WERE GOOD COMPANIONS IN BEER DRINKING AND GRASS-PUFFING AND PLANNING SESSIONS. MANY OF THESE WERE **CRACK** CHESS PLAYERS. BETWEEN OUR MEETINGS WE USED TO PLAY A **LOT** OF CHESS.

THE **HSP** RANKS WERE JOINED BY SOME STUDENTS I HAD KNOWN DURING THE PREVIOUS SCHOOL YEAR: **PAM STARR**, WHO HAD SPENT TWO YEARS AT **LUTHER**, WHERE I HAD BEEN DURING MY UNDERGRADUATE YEARS, AND WHO HAD BEEN INVOLVED IN THE ORIGINAL **LUTHER COLLEGE SDS** IN **1967; BEN KINSEY,** WHO HAD BEEN IN ONE OF MY PHILOSOPHY CLASSES WHEN I HAD BEEN WORKING IN THE PHILOSOPHY DEPARTMENT AS A TEACHING ASSISTANT AND WHO WAS WORKING HIS OWN WAY UP IN THE RANKS OF ACADEMIC PHILOSOPHY. I COULD NOT GET MY OLD **IOWA CITY** ROOMMATE TO SHARE MY VIEWS, HOWEVER. THIS WAS **STEPHEN KLOSTER,** WHO WAS EFFORTLESSLY ACQUIRING A **PH.D.** IN COMPUTER MATHEMATICS. PART OF THE WORK HE WAS DOING FOR HIS DEGREE WAS FOR A GOVERNMENT MILITARY PROJECT, AND HE FELT UNEASY AT THE PROSPECT OF SERVING TWO **OPPOSED** INTERESTS. HE WAS ALSO VERY SKEPTICAL ABOUT THE GOALS OF BOTH THE **SDS** AND THE ANARCHIST **HSP.** I WAS IN NO MOOD THEN TO SHARE HIS DETACHED ANALYSIS, THOUGH IF I HAD I WOULD HAVE BEEN A MUCH BETTER **TACTICIAN.** THAT IS SOMETHING TO REMEMBER FOR THE NEXT ROUND.

THE **PL** PEOPLE HAD MORE DIEHARDS THAN WE DID, STEADY VOTERS WHO APPEARED ON **MONDAY** NIGHTS LOOKING VERY **HUMORLESS** AND WAITING FOR THE CORRECT LINE TO PREVAIL AND FOR ALL THE **"INFANTILE LEFTISTS"** TO WITHER AWAY. WE HAD REALLY GONE BEYOND THE ANTIWAR MOVEMENT AT THAT POINT AND HAD BEGUN THE SERIOUS BUSINESS OF SORTING OUT **WHICH** BRAND OF RADICALISM WAS **LEGITIMATE.** THE PLERS HAD A FEW REAL **FANATICS** AMONG THEM: ONE WAS **BRUCE CLARK,** WHO HAD BEGUN HIS CAREER BY WEARING A BLACK ANTIWAR ARMBAND IN HIS HIGH SCHOOL IN **DES MOINES.** HE HAD LONG SINCE LEFT BEHIND SUCH **SENTIMENTAL** DISPLAYS, UNLESS IT WAS TO HAVE SOME FURTHER USE TO THE PLP. ONE OF HIS SIDEKICKS WAS A SORT OF MUSCLE MAN, UTTERLY **DEVOTED** TO THE PL LINE. WE SHALL HEAR MORE OF HIM LATER.

SOMEHOW THE **SDS** HAD GOTTEN POSSESSION OF THE **IOWA CITY** UNDERGROUND PAPER, CALLED (WHAT ELSE) **"MIDDLE EARTH."** RATHER THAN TURNING IT INTO ANOTHER VERSION OF THE BIZARRE OFFICIAL PL PAPER, WE MANAGED TO APPOINT AN EDITOR WHO STOOD ALOOF FROM OUR IDEOLOGICAL DIFFERENCES, PROBABLY BECAUSE HE DIDN'T KNOW **WHAT** THE HELL WE WERE TALKING ABOUT. HE WAS A GENIAL YOUNG MAN OF **17.** I WAS MUCH HIS SENIOR, BEING ALREADY NEAR MY MID-TWENTIES IN THOSE TIMES. I HOPED MY PRIOR EXPERIENCE WOULD CONVINCE HIM TO GIVE ME A **COLUMN** BUT THAT GOT NOWHERE. HE STARTED OFF WELL, HOWEVER, RUNNING PIECES ON THE **PEACE AND FREEDOM PARTY** AND **ELDRIDGE CLEAVER,** A MAN WE ANARCHISTS IN THE HSP TENDED TO SUPPORT, THOUGH, IDEALLY, WE SHOULD HAVE HAD NOTHING AT ALL TO DO WITH ANY SORT OF **NATIONAL** ELECTION. IN THE ACTUAL EVENT, I DID NOT VOTE AT ALL. ANYWAY, WE FELT WE HAD GOTTEN **"MIDDLE EARTH"** OFF TO A GOOD START. THE **FREAKS** WHO HUNG OUT IN THE UNION USED TO SELL IT DOWNTOWN AND GET A NICKEL FOR EACH ONE THEY SOLD. AS A MATTER OF FACT, I SOLD IT TOO WHEN A LITTLE SHY OF BEER OR FOOD MONEY.

I SHOULD MENTION MORE ABOUT THE FREAKS, THE **"DRUGGIES"** WHO MADE THE **GOLD FEATHER ROOM** SO DECORATIVE. THEY WERE OUR SHOCK TROOPS, SO TO SPEAK. THERE WILL NEVER AGAIN BE ANY GROUP COMPARABLE TO THEM. THEY WERE NOT YET SO SUNK INTO THEIR OWN MYSTICAL **GRANDEUR** THAT THEY COULD NOT BE ROUSED TO GO OUT AND DEMONSTRATE. WE WOULD LEAFLET THEM AND AGITATE THEM OR EVEN TURN OFF THE JUKEBOX IN THE UNION

CLEAVER

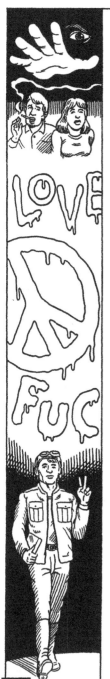

SO THEY COULD BE STIRRED UP. THESE PEOPLE, BECAUSE THEY WERE MORE **VISIBLE** THAN WE WERE, OR SO WE THOUGHT, ALWAYS TOOK THE BRUNT OF THE POLICE AND ADMINISTRATION COUNTERMEASURES. OF COURSE, THEY WERE ALWAYS BEING BUSTED FOR **DOPE** ANYWAY.

THAT SCENE IN **IOWA CITY** HAD MUCH INTENSIFIED SINCE THE PREVIOUS SPRING. SOME WHO HAD BEEN GENTLE **REEFER** TOKERS HAD GOTTEN INTO SHOOTING **SPEED**, WHICH HAD BECOME THE DRUG OF CHOICE OF THE HARDEST CORE. I HEARD THEN ABOUT VARIOUS SPECTACULARLY **BAD TIMES** PEOPLE HAD HAD COMING **DOWN** FROM SPEED OR AT THE HEIGHT OF ITS EFFECT. FOR INSTANCE, ONE POOR YOUNG MAN **CRAWLED** AROUND THE FLOOR AT PARTIES UNDER THE IMPRESSION THAT HE WAS **VOMITING** RAZORS.

I DID NOT HAVE TOO MUCH TIME FOR **MOST OF THE FREAKS**. A LOT OF THEM WERE EXCEPTIONALLY IMMATURE, WRITING THE WORDS "**LOVE**" AND "**FUCK**" ON VARIOUS WALLS ALONG WITH THE **PEACE** SYMBOL, WHICH WAS STARTING THEN TO BECOME A BIT TRITE. ALSO, A LOT OF THEM WERE SUBSIDIZED BY **WEALTHY** PARENTS WHO WERE MERELY WAITING FOR THEIR KIDS TO STRAIGHTEN UP AND GET BACK INTO PREPROFESSIONAL COURSES. A LOT OF THEM FINALLY DID, BUT IN THE MEANTIME WE WERE ABLE TO ROUSE THEM TO A FEW OF THE SOCIAL **REALITIES**. WE AS YET HAD NO COMPETITION EXCEPT FOR INTERNALLY PLACED **FBI AGENTS**.

THE SURREALIST PART OF ALL THIS WAS ALMOST ENTIRELY LEFT UP TO ME. I MADE PHOTOCOPIES OF "**LA REVOLUTION SURREALISTE**" AT THE UNIVERSITY LIBRARY AND HOPED TO TRANSLATE PASSAGES INTO ENGLISH FOR THE "**MIDDLE EARTH**" OR FOR THE "**IOWA DEFENDER**," A SLIGHTLY MORE LITERATE ANTIESTABLISHMENT PAPER. SOMEHOW I NEVER FOUND THE **LEISURE TIME** FOR THAT IN THE FALL OF '68.

I ALSO CHECKED OUT A BOOK ON **EROTIC** SURREALIST ART AND THIS AROUSED A FAIR AMOUNT OF ATTENTION, PARTICULARLY WHEN IT WAS **OBSERVED** IN A STONED CONDITION. EVEN **BILL KINSEY**, WHO WAS ALWAYS SO ANALYTICAL, BECAME **INTRIGUED** WITH THE MORE LIBIDINOUS WORK OF **DALÍ** AND THE GROTESQUE YOUNG GIRLS OF **HANS BELLMER**. IN PRACTICE, RATHER THAN THEORY AND BOOKS, I PERSONALLY TRIED TO PRESENT A **DISQUIETING** AND MIND-OPENING APPEARANCE. I PERSISTENTLY WORE KNEE-HIGH CAVALRY BOOTS AND OFTEN PLACED A PAIR OF OLD RED AVIATOR'S **GOGGLES** ATOP MY HEAD, AND I ALSO SPORTED A **WWI** TUNIC. IN THAT GARB I ATTENDED STAID UNIVERSITY LECTURES, THE MOST MEMORABLE OF WHICH DEALT WITH THE DANCE OF DEATH IN THE **LATER MIDDLE AGES**. IN THAT INSTANCE, I WAS OUTCLASSED BY THE SURREAL NATURE OF THE TOPIC.

I ALSO WROTE SURREALIST VERSE AND MADE FRIENDS WITH A YOUNG, VERY CONFUSED MAN WHO KNEW **FRANKLIN ROSEMONT** IN **CHICAGO**, THE KINGPIN OF RENASCENT **AMERICAN** SURREALISM. **ROSEMONT** HAD MET **ANDRÉ BRETON** IN **PARIS** AND SO I WAS IN A MANNER OF SPEAKING **CONNECTED** WITH THE ORIGINAL MOVEMENT. MY NEW FRIEND DID NOT REALLY HAVE AN ATTACHMENT TO ANY PARTICULAR "**ISM**." HE THOUGHT OF HIMSELF MOSTLY AS A **YIPPIE** AND DID THINGS LIKE BURNING DOLLAR BILLS TO PROTEST CAPITALISM, ETC., WHICH ALWAYS INFURIATED THE PL PEOPLE, WHO FELT THAT **EVERY** DOLLAR SHOULD GO FOR THE ULTIMATE **TRIUMPH** OF THE **PROLETARIAT**. HE ALSO FELT THAT THE **SOVIET** INTERVENTION IN **CZECHOSLOVAKIA** WAS JUSTIFIED BECAUSE **FIDEL CASTRO** THOUGHT SO. I WARMLY DISAGREED WITH HIM ON THAT POINT. IT WAS, HOWEVER, GOOD TO HAVE HIM AROUND

DALI

BECAUSE HIS UNPREDICTABLE AND DRAMATIC ACTIONS AND IMAGINATIVE PROFANITY **ATTRACTED** THE CROWDS WE COULD NOT OURSELVES GATHER.

I CONTINUED TO READ HEAVILY INTO SURREALISM AND I TRIED TO INCORPORATE ITS BELIEF IN THE **FREEDOM** OF THOUGHT, ITS RELIANCE ON THE PENUMBRAL **DREAMWORLD** AND THE BEAUTY IT SOUGHT TO FIND IN **CHANCE** AND **SPONTANEITY**. **IOWA CITY** BEGAN TO BE A PLACE OF GRAND MYSTERY, WHERE MAD LOVE AND **MADDER** POETRY SEEMED POSSIBLE. IT DID NOT SEEM PROBABLE, HOWEVER. MOST OF MY ACQUAINTANCES THERE, EVEN THE **DRUG** PEOPLE, WERE PRETTY PROSAIC. IT WAS JUST SOMETHING IN THE AIR OF THAT **SEPTEMBER** THAT WAS DEFINITELY AND STRANGELY CONDUCIVE TO MY DESIRE FOR **CONTACT** WITH THE **MARVELOUS**.

WE FINALLY WERE CONVINCED THAT **SDS** WOULD NEVER MAKE A MOVE. SO WE VOTED TO HAVE AN **HSP** RALLY ON THE STEPS OF THE OLD CAPITOL. THIS WAS IN THE MIDDLE OF **SEPTEMBER**. THE **U. OF I.** ADMINISTRATORS HAD DECIDED TO MAKE RALLIES THERE **ILLEGAL**, SO WE DECIDED TO HOLD ONE TO CHALLENGE THAT BIT OF ASININITY. ON **WEDNESDAY** THE 18TH, WE GATHERED ON THOSE STEPS AND UNDER THE PORTICO AND BEGAN TO SPEAK. DRS. **ADDISS** AND **BAKER** OF THE PHILOSOPHY DEPARTMENT APPEARED TO URGE US TO OPERATE IN A **LEGAL** FRAMEWORK. THEIR CAUSE, HOWEVER, WAS NOT OURS. THEY WERE VINTAGE **PACIFISTS** AND WE WANTED **ACTION**. WE KEPT ON TALKING, AND GROUPS OF LISTENERS CAME AND WENT. THE ADMINISTRATORS PRESENT CONFINED THEMSELVES TO WATCHING. SO DID SOME OF THE **PL-SDS** MEMBERS, WHO SEEMED PUZZLED AND AMUSED. WE HAD NEVERTHELESS STOLEN A **MARCH** ON THEM, AND THE "**DAILY IOWAN**," THE OFFICIAL STUDENT NEWSPAPER, GAVE US GOOD COVERAGE THE NEXT DAY. **JERRY SIES** WAS MENTIONED BY NAME. THEY **KNEW** WHO HE WAS. THE REST OF US **REMAINED** AS AN UNKNOWN AND DISQUIETING ELEMENT.

THE NEXT NIGHT A FEW OF US MET IN **THE MILL**. THIS WAS THE BAR THAT WAS FAVORED BY **FREAKS** AND **ACTIVISTS**. THE OWNER WAS SOMETHING OF A BOHEMIAN BUT **NOT** A LEFTIST BY ANY MEANS. HE SOMETIMES MOCKED US BY SINGING: "THE WORKING CLASS CAN KISS MY **ASS**. I'VE GOT THE BOSS'S JOB AT **LAST**." HE LET US **CASH** OUR DUBIOUS CHECKS THERE, SO WE MANAGED TO GET ALONG. THE WAITERS WERE ALL DOCTORAL CANDIDATES, APPARENTLY. THE PLACE HAS SLIPPED IN THESE **LATTER** DAYS. ON MOST NIGHTS THE CROWDED **MILL** WAS FILLED WITH MUSIC FROM LIVE FOLK-SINGERS, SOMETIMES A **JUG** BAND, SOMETIMES A LONG-HAIRED BROWN-EYED GIRL GIVING A SERIES OF HAUNTING BALLADS ALL SHE HAD, WHICH WAS CONSIDERABLE.

THE BEER WASN'T BAD EITHER, AND WE CONSUMED QUITE A LOT OF IT WHILE THINKING OF WAYS TO GET ACROSS OUR POINT OF VIEW. FINALLY WE HIT UPON THE IDEA OF USING **GUERRILLA THEATER**. **BOB ECKHART** GOT HOLD OF A MOTORCYCLE HELMET THAT LOOKED LIKE THE HEADPIECES WORN BY THE **CHICAGO** POLICE, AND HE GAVE IT TO **KEN WESSELS**, THE VETERAN **HSP** MEMBER, WHO WAS TO PORTRAY A POLICEMAN. BOB PORTRAYED A STUDENT RADICAL AND I PORTRAYED A MEMBER OF THE **PROGRESSIVE LABOR PARTY**. WE SET UP A SPEAKER'S PODIUM IN THE UNION NEAR THE **GOLD FEATHER ROOM**, AND **BOB** BEGAN TO SPEAK. THEN **KEN**, SHOUTING SOME QUITE CONVINCING **OBSCENITIES**, CHARGED AT HIM WAVING AN IMPROVISED RIOT CLUB. BY SOME STRETCH OF OUR IMAGINATIONS, WE GOT THE FICTITIOUS POLICEMAN TO LISTEN TO **BOB**, AND HE MANAGED TO CONVINCE **KEN** THAT HE SHOULD

165

SIDE WITH US SINCE, AFTER ALL, WE WERE ON THE SIDE OF THE WORKING CLASS AND SO FORTH. THEN I GOT UP AND DID MY **PL** IMPERSONATION, SAYING THINGS LIKE, "OH, BUT YOU WERE NOT FOLLOWING THE **CORRECT** LINE," OR "GOODNESS, WHERE DOES IT **MENTION** THIS IN THE WORKS OF **LENIN?**"

THAT EVENING, IN ONE OF THE DREADFUL HAMBURGER **JOINTS** THAT PROBABLY STILL FLOURISH IN **IOWA CITY,** A GRADUATE STUDENT RADICAL MUTTERED THAT I WAS WASHING "OUR **DIRTY** LAUNDRY IN PUBLIC." I ASKED HIM IF HE FAVORED A PRIVATE **PURGE** INSTEAD, WHICH ONLY MADE HIM MUTTER ALL THE MORE. WE DEFINITELY **WEREN'T** "GETTING OUR SHIT TOGETHER."

AT ABOUT THIS POINT, **PAM STARR** AND **BEN KINSEY** DECIDED TO RETURN TO PURE ACADEMICS, WHICH WAS ALL RIGHT FOR **PAM.** LAST I HEARD SHE WAS IN MED SCHOOL AND HOPING TO WORK IN AN ALL-FEMALE **CLINIC,** FREE OF MALE PATERNALISM, ETC. I LIKED HER AND WAS SORRY TO SEE HER LEAVE THE RANKS OF ACTIVISTS. WE WENT ON WITHOUT THEM, FEARING **NOTHING** AT ALL. IN THOSE DAYS, I WASN'T EVEN SCARED OF **PRISON,** EVEN THOUGH I PROBABLY WOULD HAVE HAD A HELLISH TIME HAD I BEEN THROWN IN AMONG THE **WOLVES.**

THE **MONDAY** AFTER THE **HSP** RALLY, **SDS** DECIDED TO HOLD ONE ALSO. WE WERE **OVERJOYED** AND DECIDED TO MINIMIZE OUR DIFFERENCES WITH THE **PL** FACTION IN THE GREATER INTEREST OF SOLIDARITY. THE ADMINISTRATORS BY NOW HAD A QUITE REASONABLE (FROM THEIR VIEWPOINT) **DISLIKE** OF **SDS** AND THEY REALLY DIDN'T LIKE THAT GATHERING. NEARLY EVERY MEMBER SPOKE AND THE ANARCHISTS AIRED THEIR VIEWS. THE MEMBERS OF THE STUDENT AUDIENCE WERE INVITED UP TO THE MICROPHONE, AND THEY BEGAN DENOUNCING VARIOUS **POLICIES** OF THE UNIVERSITY AND OF THE **U.S.A.,** SOMETIMES IN TERMS EVEN HARSHER THAN THOSE WE HAD USED. IT WAS A GREAT **SUCCESS.** IT ALSO GOT THE **SDS** IN HOT WATER. A UNIVERSITY COMMITTEE BEGAN TO DETERMINE WHETHER THE **SDS** COULD STILL BE CONSIDERED A CAMPUS ORGANIZATION IN VIEW OF ITS FLOUTING OF SCHOOL **REGULATIONS.** WE **HSP** MEMBERS WERE HURT. THE ACADEMIC SATRAPS STILL MADE NO MENTION OF OUR RALLY THE PREVIOUS WEEK. WE WERE **IGNORED,** NOT A GREAT EXPERIENCE FOR ACTIVE ANARCHISTS. WE PLANNED TO DO BETTER AS **SOON** AS WE COULD.

BEFORE I COULD DO ANY MORE FOR THE ANARCHIST IDEAL, THE SURREALIST HALF OF MY IDEOLOGY CAME OUT OF THE NIGHT IN PURE CHANCE AND IRONY AND **BLEW ME AWAY.** I HAD GONE TO **THE MILL,** WHICH SOMEHOW I HAD CONFUSED WITH THE "**RED MILL,**" A LIGHT OPERA BY **VICTOR HERBERT.** I ALWAYS WROTE MY CHECKS OUT TO THE "**RED MILL.**" THAT NIGHT, **SEPTEMBER 23,** WAS QUIET. IT WAS SO QUIET IN FACT THAT I TOOK THE ACOUSTIC GUITAR THAT THEY RESERVED FOR MUSICAL PATRONS AND BEGAN TO PICK OUT A FEW CHORDS OF A **BEACH BOYS** TUNE. A FRIEND OF MINE CAME IN, ORDERED A BEER, AND SAT DOWN NEXT TO ME. THEN WE BOTH NOTICED TWO GIRLS WHO HAD JUST COME IN. WE **JOINED** THEM AND I BROUGHT THE GUITAR WITH ME. IN **1968** PLAYING A FEW TUNES ON A GUITAR WAS STILL A **GOOD** ICEBREAKER. LATER ON, THE WORDS BEGAN TO STICK IN OUR THROATS. I PLAYED THEM MY VERSION OF **DION AND THE BELMONTS'** "TEENAGER IN LOVE," WHICH I CALLED "**DRAFT DODGER IN JAIL.**" THE GIRLS WERE AMUSED BY US AND WE WERE INVITED TO THEIR APARTMENT, ACTUALLY ONE-HALF OF A SMALL ONE-STORY HOUSE. I BOUGHT A SIX-PACK OF BEER TO TAKE ALONG THAT I DIDN'T **NEED,** AS IT TURNED OUT. THE GIRLS HAD SOME QUALITY **WEED** FROM **CALIFORNIA** FRIENDS AND OFFERED

US SOME. IT WAS ABSOLUTELY THE **STRONGEST** STUFF I EVER SMOKED. IT WAS WHAT WE LATER ON TERMED "**TWO-TOKE STUFF.**" I HAD NEVER RUN INTO **ANYTHING** LIKE IT. I HAD ALSO NEVER RUN INTO **ANYONE** LIKE THE GIRL WHO WAS SHARING A JOINT WITH ME.

"A VERY YOUNG, VERY UNHAPPY WOMAN, HAVING ON HER SIDE THE TWILIGHT **BEAUTY** OF BEINGS WHO GIVE THEMSELVES, WHO **ABANDON** THEMSELVES BECAUSE IT IS **THUS** THAT THEY SHALL UNDO HIM WHO **RECEIVES** THEM."
-PAUL ELUARD (1930)

WE **HELD** HANDS AT FIRST. SUDDENLY IT SEEMED AS THOUGH SOMEONE HAD **FUSED** OUR CIRCUITS AND JAMMED OUR CHEMICAL BONDS TOGETHER, HAD LIT EVENING FLARES AND PRODDED OPEN THE DRAGON-GUARDED GATES OF THE **MARVELOUS.** IT WAS AS STARTLING AS IT WAS PLEASURABLE AND AS DISTURBING AS IT WAS AMAZING. MY RADICAL FRIEND SEEMED TO **VANISH** AND MY **SEPTEMBER** APPARITION, **ELIZABETH ANNE KATHERINE,** UNDRESSED WHILE I LAY NEXT TO HER, STUPEFIED BY THE **GRASS** I HAD SMOKED. LUCKILY I WAS NOT COMPLETELY IMMOBILIZED. MUCH LATER, STRANGELY COLORED NUMBERS AND SCENES WERE **STILL** RUNNING THROUGH MY HEAD, RIGHT IN THE BACKS OF MY EYES.

HER SEXUAL **READINESS** JOLTED SOME OF THE OLD PRECONCEPTIONS I HAD OF WOMEN INTO OBLIVION. **BETTEANNE** WAS THE NAME SHE PREFERRED. SHE WAS FROM **CHICAGO,** A UNIVERSITY SOPHOMORE WHO HOPED TO GET A **B.A.** IN ORIENTAL RELIGION. NO ONE WHO **WORRIES** ABOUT A **MONEY** SUPPLY GETS A MAJOR IN ANYTHING LIKE THAT, AND THAT WAS TRUE IN HER CASE. HER FATHER WAS A VICE PRESIDENT OF SOMETHING LIKE THE **"SCREW CORPORATION,"** I SWEAR TO IT.

SHE WAS **NOT** A SMALL GIRL. SHE WAS ABOUT **5'7"** AND WAS **SHAPELY** AND DECEPTIVELY STURDY IN APPEARANCE. FROM HER MOTHER'S SIDE OF THE FAMILY SHE HAD INHERITED BROWN EYES AND A FAINT RESEMBLANCE TO **JOAN BAEZ.** SHE HAD BEEN RIGOROUSLY RAISED AS A **CATHOLIC** ALTHOUGH SHE HAD BECOME AN APOSTATE. HER VOICE COMBINED THE HARSHNESS OF **CHICAGO** WITH A PECULIAR MUSICAL STRAIN THAT I WILL WAIT IN VAIN TO HEAR FROM **ANYONE** ELSE. WE WERE **ENGAGED** TO BE MARRIED AFTER WE HAD BEEN TOGETHER FOR TWO WEEKS. I HAD NOT SOLD OUT SURREALISM BY ANY MEANS. THE GREAT SURREALIST FIGURES HAD ALWAYS HAD ONE GREAT, IDEALIZED LOVE PARTNER IN THEIR LIVES, THOUGH, ADMITTEDLY, THE IDENTITY OF THE WIFE OR LOVER WAS SUBJECT TO CHANGE THROUGH A PROCESS OF EXALTED **SERIAL MONOGAMY.**

IN A FEW DAYS WE HAD **ANOTHER** RALLY IN FRONT OF THE OLD CAPITOL. THIS TIME I REMEMBERED TO BRING MY BLACK ANARCHIST FLAG WITH ME. **PAUL McKIBBEN** AND I ALTERNATELY BRANDISHED IT ALOFT ON THE OLD STEPS TO AN **EVEN** MIXTURE OF CHEERS AND HISSING. THE **SDS PLERS** DID THE HISSING, WHICH GAVE THE EVENT THE CHARACTER OF AN OLD-TIME MELODRAMA. THE **"DES MOINES REGISTER"** GOT A PICTURE OF THIS RALLY, BLACK FLAG AND ALL, AND RAN IT ON THE FRONT PAGE, OR SO I WAS **TOLD.** I WAS TOO DISTRACTED **THEN** TO REMEMBER TO GET A COPY.

MOST EVENINGS I SPENT WITH **BETTEANNE,** LISTENING TO RECORDS, DRINKING WINE, ENJOYING GRASS AND HER, AND SPOUTING **POLITICAL** THEORY AND TACTICS. SHE WASN'T REALLY VERY INTERESTED IN EITHER **SDS** OR THE **HSP.** SHE WAS A STUDENT OF EASTERN RELIGIONS AND WAS AT THAT TIME STUDYING

ELUARD

BUDDHISM AND CONFUCIANISM. SHE HAD ALSO ADOPTED BEATLE-STYLE THOUGHT ABOUT AHIMSA, INNER PEACE, THAT SORT OF THING. I HAD NO TIME FOR SUCH A WORLDVIEW THAT FALL BUT I NEVER CALLED HER ON IT. WE MERELY DRIFTED ALONG INTO THE BEAUTIFUL AUTUMN OF 1968. I HAD NEVER SEEN IOWA CITY MORE LOVELY. WE WALKED DOWN BY THE IOWA RIVER, NEAR THE UNION, AND OFTEN STOPPED TO REST THERE AMONG THE LEAVES IN THE EARLY EVENING, HOLDING EACH OTHER CLOSELY IN THE EROTIC, SPECTRAL HALF-LIGHT.

THIS WAS THE HIGH POINT. MY OWN ASPIRATIONS FOR A WORLD TRANSFIGURED BY MAD LOVE AND POLITICAL ANARCHISM SEEMED AT SUCH TIMES TO BE ALMOST WITHIN REACH. BETTEANNE WAS RADIANT WITH DESIRE AND ITS FULFILLMENT, AND MY RADICAL FRIENDS WERE FULL OF CONFIDENCE. NOTHING WE DID SEEMED TO BE AN ERROR. THE ADMINISTRATION OF THE UNIVERSITY WAS AT A LOSS AS TO HOW TO DEAL WITH US. I CAN'T REALLY PINPOINT THE EXACT BEGINNING OF OUR RUIN. THE SEEDS, HOWEVER, WERE THERE, EVEN IN THE HSP ITSELF.

A NUMBER OF THE MEMBERS HAD BEGUN TO MAKE SOME SPARE CHANGE BY DEALING IN MARIJUANA. I OBJECTED TO THIS AND SAID THEY WERE ONLY MAKING THEMSELVES SITTING DUCKS FOR THE FBI OR THE CIA OR THE REGULAR OLD IOWA CITY POLICE. THE IOWA CITY JAIL HELD LOTS OF DRUGGIES IN THOSE DAYS. WE SOMETIMES TRIED TO COMMUNICATE WITH THEM THROUGH THE BARS, BUT THE COPS ALWAYS CHASED US WELL OUT OF EARSHOT. THE DEALERS PAID NO ATTENTION TO ME BUT PURSUED THEIR NOCTURNAL BUSINESS. THOSE WHO WERE IN THE HSP AND SDS OFTEN SHOWED UP IMPOSSIBLY STONED. IN THE LATTER CASE IT WAS PARTICULARLY UNFORTUNATE BECAUSE THE LIBERTARIANS IN SDS NEEDED TO HAVE ALL THEIR WITS ABOUT THEM. THE PROGRESSIVE LABOR FACTION, ALL OF WHOM WERE STRAIGHT AND MORALISTIC, CONTINUED TO DOMINATE THE MEETINGS. I JOINED WITH PL ON THE OCCASION TO LEAFLET AN IOWA CITY HIGH SCHOOL IN ORDER TO HAVE MORE YOUNG PEOPLE ATTEND OUR SDS-SPONSORED MOVIES. WE HAD MOVIES ON THE UPRISING AT COLUMBIA UNIVERSITY AND ON THE BLACK PANTHERS (CHEERS FOR CLEAVER) AND THE NATIONAL LIBERATION FRONT IN VIETNAM AND FELT THEY NEEDED TO BE SEEN. A YOUNG BEARDED SCHOOLTEACHER PROMPTLY INFORMED HIS PRINCIPAL, WHO INFORMED US THAT HE WOULD INFORM THE POLICE. SO OUR BRAINS INFORMED OUR FEET TO GET MOVING. WE HAD ONLY DISTRIBUTED SEVERAL DOZEN LEAFLETS.

DRUG USE WAS NOT CONFINED TO ILLEGAL SUBSTANCES. BETTEANNE HAD SOME SINISTER ORANGE PILLS KNOWN AS AMBAR, A COMBINATION OF AMPHETAMINES AND BARBITURATES. I DISCOVERED THAT SHE TOOK THEM WITH GREAT REGULARITY AND ALSO HAD A REFILLABLE PRESCRIPTION FOR THEM. I TRIED ONE ONCE AND STAYED UP ALL ONE OCTOBER NIGHT AND WROTE FIFTY PAGES OF A NOVEL I WAS WORKING ON THEN IN WHATEVER SPARE TIME I HAD. THE NEXT DAY I "CAME DOWN" AND FELL SOUNDLY ASLEEP IN THE MIDDLE OF THE AFTERNOON, NOT WAKING UNTIL THE NEXT MORNING. I WASTED NO TIME IN TELLING HER TO QUIT USING AMBAR, BUT LIKE MY FRIENDS IN THE HSP, SHE PAID NO ATTENTION TO MY WARNINGS. I MYSELF HAD A JOINT NOW AND THEN, BUT MY PRIMARY MOOD-ALTERING WAS DONE WITH BEER IN THE OLD MILL.

SOME OF THE HSP PEOPLE GOT INTO ACID-TRIPPING. THIS REALLY BOTHERED ME. THEY WOULD BE OUT OF TOUCH FOR DAYS. THEY SEEMED TO BE DRIFTING DOWN TOWARD THE SPEED SUBCULTURE THAT OFTEN SURFACED IN THE GOLD FEATHER ROOM OR IN THE

MILL, A GROUP OF RAGGED, GREEN-GRAY PEOPLE WITH MEMORABLE FIXED AND EERIE **STARES**. PEOPLE SEEMED TO SHRINK DOWN FROM AMPHETAMINES BEFORE YOUR VERY EYES. THERE WAS ALSO A LOT OF TALK ABOUT "MESC" AND PSILOCYBIN. I HAVE SERIOUS DOUBTS IF ANYTHING EXCEPT THE USUAL ANIMAL TRANQUILIZERS EVER GOT INGESTED IN **IOWA CITY** EXCEPT POSSIBLY IN THE VERY **EARLY** FREAK ERA THERE, IN LATE '66 AND EARLY '67. I RESENTED THE FACT THAT THE **HSP** PEOPLE WERE MIXING IN WITH THE DRUGGIES' LOW COMMON DENOMINATOR. IT SEEMED TO HAPPEN VERY QUICKLY, BUT IT STILL WAS NOT A SERIOUS PHENOMENON. THE **HSP**ERS STILL TURNED OUT FOR THE RALLIES. THERE WAS A GOOD ONE IN THE MIDDLE OF **OCTOBER** ON A VERY FINE DAY. WE WERE GETTING USED TO **SPLENDID** WEATHER. ONCE AGAIN WE HAD AUDIENCE PARTICIPATION AND THE AROUSED STUDENTS MARCHED UP TO THE MIKE IN TURN. ONE OF THEM INTRODUCED HIMSELF AS **SKY KING** AND CARRIED ON A BIZARRE AIR-TO-GROUND CONVERSATION. I WAS ON AFTER HIM AND INTRODUCED MYSELF AS MY SOCIAL SECURITY NUMBER, AND TOLD ABOUT HOW HAPPY AND WELL-ADJUSTED I WAS IN THE NEW **ORDERLY** SOCIETY AND HOW I WAS GOING TO FILL MY NICHE IN AN OFFICIALLY **APPROVED** MANNER. I WENT ON LIKE THAT FOR A WHILE BEFORE I WAS AWARE OF A HAND TAPPING MY SHOULDER. IT WAS ONE OF THE SCHOOL OFFICIALS, **ROGER AUGUSTINE**, WHO DEMANDED TO KNOW MY NAME AND STUDENT ID NUMBER IN ACCORDANCE WITH A NEW REPRESSIVE REGULATION THAT HAD COME INTO FORCE IN THE SUMMER, WHEN THE RADICALS HAD BEEN IN **CHICAGO** OR POINTS WEST. IN KEEPING WITH MY DESIRE FOR ANONYMITY I **DECLINED** TO IDENTIFY MYSELF. I TURNED AROUND AND ASKED HIM WHO HE WAS. HE REPEATED HIS DEMAND AND GOT VERY RED-FACED. I TOLD HIM I WASN'T A STUDENT. THEN HE WAS SURROUNDED BY **SIES** AND OTHER DEMONSTRATORS WHO WARMLY OBJECTED TO HIS INTRUSION. WHAT I REMEMBER **MOST** FROM THAT PARTICULAR RALLY WAS THE LAUGHTER AND APPLAUSE THAT GREETED MY NUMERICAL FANTASY. EVEN SOME OF THE TOUGHER PLERS WERE **ALMOST** COMPLIMENTARY.

I WAS PLEASED AT THE COMPLIMENT, CONSIDERING THE SOURCE. WE MUST HAVE FINALLY MADE SOME IMPRESSION ON THE **RIVAL** FACTION IN OUR **SDS** BECAUSE AT LAST THEY DECIDED TO JOIN ONE OF OUR DEMONSTRATIONS, ONE WE HAD LINED UP TO OPPOSE THE **DOW CHEMICAL COMPANY** RECRUITERS EARLY IN **NOVEMBER**. THUS, FOR THE FIRST TIME THAT SEMESTER THE CAMPUS **MAOISTS** AND ANARCHISTS GOT TOGETHER ON SOMETHING AS A UNITED GROUP. **BRUCE CLARK, PAT KEARNY**, ANOTHER **HSP** MEMBER, POSSIBLY **WESSELS**, AND I SAT DOWN AND DRAFTED A LEAFLET. IT WAS RATHER CLEAR AND NOT OVERLY RHETORICAL IN PUTTING OUR CASE AGAINST THE NAPALM-MAKERS. THE ONLY INTEMPERANCE WAS PERHAPS THE SMALL **SWASTIKA** WE PLACED INSIDE THE "O" IN **DOW**. WE HIT THE STREETS AND LEAFLETED LIKE CRAZY, THOUGH THE WINDS WERE A BIT COLDER AS **OCTOBER** DREW ON.

DURING THAT MONTH, THE NEW **BEATLES** ALBUM HAD COME OUT, THE ONE WITH THE TWO RECORDS IN THE WHITE ALBUM COVER, THE ONE THAT CONTAINED **MANSON'S** FUTURE THEME SONG, "HELTER SKELTER." SOME OF THE YOUTHFUL "MIDDLE EARTH" STAFFERS SET TO WORK REVIEWING IT, AND IT GOT A BIG SPREAD IN THE NEXT ISSUE OF THE UNDERGROUND PAPER. A LITTLE DISPROPORTIONATE, I THOUGHT, FOR WHAT SHOULD HAVE BEEN THE GOALS OF THE PAPER; THAT IS TO PROMOTE RADICALISM AND NOT TO DRAW **MORE** ATTENTION TO RICH EGO-TRIPPING MUSICIANS, DITTO FOR **DYLAN** AND **THE STONES**, ESPECIALLY **THE STONES**, WHO WERE AT THAT TIME GREASING THE SKIDS FOR **BRIAN JONES**.

169

#9

ONE OF THE NUMBERS ON THE NEW **BEATLES** ALBUM WAS **"REVOLUTION NUMBER NINE."** WE LISTENED TO **THAT** OVER AND OVER, BACKWARD AND FORWARD, STONED, DRUNK, OR SOBER, AND TRIED TO FIND OUT WHAT CLUES IT WOULD GIVE US, IF ANY. **BETTEANNE** LISTENED TO IT STONED AND THOUGHT IT WAS VERY FUNNY. I WAS NOT AS AMUSED. SHE HAD STARTED GETTING STONED A LITTLE **TOO** OFTEN AND, WHAT WAS WORSE, DID SO WHEN I WAS NOT SMOKING WITH HER. SHE RELENTED AND LET ME TAKE **CHARGE** OF THE POTENT GRASS SHE WAS USING. I MADE A JAY OR TWO AND THEN TUCKED IT AWAY IN MY CLOSET FOR FUTURE REFERENCE. I BROUGHT ONE OF THE REEFERS OVER TO **SIES'S** PLACE. HE ALWAYS HAD WONDERED ABOUT THE **MAGICAL** WEED I KEPT TALKING ABOUT. IT HIT US AT ONCE. "JESUS CHRIST, WHAT **IS** THAT STUFF?" HE ASKED. I WAS **AMAZED.** I THOUGHT HE WOULD TELL **ME.**

THE ELECTION DREW NEARER. I HAD DEFINITELY DECIDED TO EXPRESS MY ANARCHIST OPINIONS BY BOYCOTTING IT. I DID HAVE SOME SECOND THOUGHTS AFTER MAKING THAT DECISION. THE **PEACE AND FREEDOM PARTY** NEEDED VOTES FOR **CLEAVER** AND IT ALSO HAD SOME LOCAL CANDIDATES: THE POET **MIKE LALLY,** FOR ONE, WHO WAS RUNNING FOR **JOHNSON COUNTY SHERIFF.** HE TOOK IT, AS HE DID MOST THINGS, QUITE SERIOUSLY, AND HE ACTIVELY CAMPAIGNED. **LALLY** ALSO HELPED US AT OUR RALLIES BY COMING FORWARD AND SPEAKING, ALTHOUGH HE SEEMED TO ALIGN HIMSELF MORE WITH THE ORTHODOX **MARXISTS** THAN WITH US **"CRAZIES."**

HE ALSO JOINED WITH US IN PROTESTING THE REMOVAL OF THE **"GRAFFITI BOARD"** FROM THE **GOLD FEATHER ROOM.** THIS HAD BEEN A SORT OF ROOM DIVIDER THAT PEOPLE HAD BEGUN WRITING ON WITH MAGIC MARKERS. A LOT OF EXTREMELY **WITTY** THINGS, NOT OBSCENE EITHER, HAD APPEARED, ONLY TO BE COVERED BY **FRESH** PAINT. THEN MORE OF THEM APPEARED. IT GOT BETTER FROM WEEK TO WEEK. ONE **RECURRING** FEATURE WAS A PARODY OF SOME SEMILITERATE RIGHT-WINGER WHO PURPORTEDLY WOULD WRITE THINGS LIKE: "SHUTE **ALL** COMMUNSTS AND BURID IN THE CITY DUMP LIKE DOGS." THE AUTHORITIES FINALLY RESOLVED TO HIT **BACK** AT US BY REMOVING OUR WALL. ONE NIGHT THE UNION WORKERS CAME IN, AND ONE OR TWO OF THEM HAD **ACETYLENE** TORCHES. WE TRIED TO RALLY AROUND THE VANISHING WALL, BUT THE UNION ADMINISTRATORS CLOSED THE PLACE UP EARLY AND PREVAILED UPON US TO **LEAVE.** WE DID AND TOOK THE LAST THIRD OF THE "WALL" WITH US, COMPLETE WITH **CHOICE** COMMENTS, AND LEFT IT LEANING ON THE FRONT DOOR OF THE UNIVERSITY PRESIDENT'S HOUSE. THAT WAS **HOWARD BOWEN,** A SMALL, RATHER WORRIED-LOOKING MAN WHOM **JERRY SIES** KEPT TRYING TO PUT UNDER CITIZEN'S ARREST FOR COMPLICITY IN AN **ILLEGAL** WAR. **BOWEN'S** OFFICE WAS ALSO IN THE OLD CAPITOL, WHICH WE OFTEN BESIEGED.

THE USE OF SPEED WAS SPREADING. A GIRL FROM **OMAHA** WHO HAD SOMETIMES ATTENDED **SDS** MEETINGS IN **SEPTEMBER** NOW HAD COMPLETELY FALLEN IN WITH THE AMPHETAMINE SUBCULTURE. MANY OF THEM LIVED ON THE UPPER FLOORS OF AN OLD BUILDING THAT HOUSED A **BURGER KING** RESTAURANT DOWNTOWN. ONE NIGHT I FOUND MYSELF THERE WITH THEM. **BETTEANNE** HAD GONE TO THE HOSPITAL AFTER SUFFERING REAL OR IMAGINARY **ABDOMINAL PAINS** AND HAD HAD HER APPENDIX REMOVED. SHE WAS BEGINNING TO HAVE ALL KINDS OF PAIN AND FEARS. I FIGURED IT WAS HER OLD **CATHOLIC** SENSE OF **GUILT** FINALLY CATCHING UP TO HER THAT WAS PARTLY RESPONSIBLE. ANYWAY, I COULDN'T SEE HER THAT NIGHT SO I VISITED THE SPEED **FREAKS** INSTEAD. I WAS QUITE STONED, AND I KNEW ANYONE COULD "CRASH" WITH THEM. I WAS VERY **PARANOID,** THOUGH. MOST EVERYONE WAS TRIPPING AND/OR

SPEEDING AND LISTENING TO SOMETHING ABOUT "I AM THE GOD OF **HELLFIRE**" OVER AND OVER. I FINALLY FELL ASLEEP AND IN THE MORNING WAS AWAKENED BY A VERY OFFICIAL KNOCK. IT WAS A DE-TECTIVE LIEUTENANT AND A SERGEANT, AS IT TURNED OUT. THEY WERE AFTER ONE OF THE SPEED FREAKS WHO HAD **STOLEN** A GRO-CERY STORE'S PAYROLL CHECKS, WITH THE CONNIVANCE OF ONE OF THE GIRLS PRESENT. AFTER THE **GUILTY** (ALLEGED) PARTIES HAD BEEN MADE TO VANISH, I BOUGHT A RED ROSE WITH MY FEW REMAIN-ING COINS AND BROUGHT IT OVER TO **BETTEANNE** AT THE HOSPITAL, WHERE I SAT AND WATCHED HER SLEEP.

IT WAS AT **THAT** POINT, JUST A FEW DAYS BEFORE THE ELECTIONS, THAT **"MIDDLE EARTH"** CAME TO GRIEF. ITS EDITOR HAD DECIDED TO ESCHEW POLITICS IN THE LATEST ISSUES. AS I MENTIONED, HE NEVER WAS MUCH INTO RADICALISM ANYWAY. HE CAME OUT WITH AN EDITORIAL THAT DENOUNCED **ALL POLITICS** AND INSTEAD ASKED THAT WE ACCEPT **LOVE** AS THE ANSWER. THAT WAS ALL VERY WELL FOR HIM. HE WAS A HANDSOME YOUNG BRUTE AND HAD BEEN GETTING INTO THE DRAWERS OF MOST OF THE FEMALE CONTRIBUTORS. IT WAS NOT AT ALL WELL FOR US OR FOR THE **PROGRESSIVE LABOR** FACTION. ONE OF THEM, THE MUSCLE MAN AND LOYAL FOLLOWER I MENTIONED **EARLIER**, APPROACHED THE JOURNALIST OF LOVE AND DEMANDED THE **COPY** FOR THE NEXT ISSUE. IT WAS, AFTER ALL, **SDS** MONEY THAT WAS SUPPORTING THE PAPER. THE YOUNG EDITOR **RE-FUSED** TO DO SO. THIS WAS NOT ACCEPTABLE TO THE **MAOIST,** AND HE PUNCHED THE EDITOR TO THE FLOOR, GRABBED THE COPY, PLATES, AND SO FORTH, AND **LEFT**. THE IDEALISTIC EDITOR ALSO LEFT. IN FACT, HE LEFT THE STATE AFTER WITHDRAWING ALL THE **"MIDDLE EARTH"** FUNDS FROM THE BANK. THAT WAS PROBABLY THE LAST GASP OF **FLOWER POWER** ON THE **IOWA** CAMPUS. RADICALISM IT-SELF HAD NOT MUCH LONGER TO LIVE. **NIXON** HAD BEEN ELECTED. WE HAD NEVER COUNTED ON **THAT**. THE ATMOSPHERE SEEMED TO BECOME ABOUT FIFTY DEGREES COLDER, AND THE **DOW CHEMICAL** DEMON-STRATION WE HAD PLANNED WAS A TERRIBLE **FLOP**. JUST TEN OF US STOOD THERE IN THE CHILLY DRIZZLE ALONG WITH A SYMPATHETIC **RABBI,** WHILE THE REST OF THE WORLD ALLOWED **DOW** TO GO ABOUT ITS **DEADLY** BUSINESS. NEVERTHELESS, THE UNIVERSITY ADMINIS-TRATORS WERE NOT UNDERESTIMATING US. THEY AND SOME CAMPUS POLICE STOOD INSIDE THE UNION AND BALEFULLY WATCHED US. I WENT BACK TO MY LITTLE RENTED ROOM AFTERWARD AND **WEPT**. I NO LONGER WANTED TO ADD MY PROBLEMS TO THE MANY THAT I NOW KNEW **BETTEANNE** SUFFERED FROM.

THIS WAS NOT **QUITE** THE LAST ACT OF THE ANARCHIST **HSP**. WE SCHEDULED ONE MORE MEETING AFTER THE **DOW** DEBACLE. FIVE OF US SHOWED UP AND SAT AROUND AWHILE. A REPORTER FROM THE **"DAILY IOWAN"** CAME AND ASKED US WHAT WE WERE PLANNING. THIS WAS THE FIRST TIME THAT SEMESTER THAT A REPORTER FROM THE OF-FICIAL STUDENT NEWSPAPER HAD ATTENDED OUR MEETING. SOMEHOW THE REPORTER GOT THE IDEA THAT WE WERE BEING IRONIC, "FUNNY," AND SHE SMILED. WE VOTED **UNANIMOUSLY** TO CONDEMN **RICHARD NIXON,** DECLARING THAT WE DID NOT TRUST HIM AND **NEVER** WOULD. THE REPORTER LAUGHED ALOUD. THIS WAS AMUSING, SHE PROBABLY THOUGHT, BUT NOT WORTH A STORY. THEN WE VOTED UNANIMOUSLY TO DISSOLVE THE **HAWKEYE STUDENT PARTY** AND TO CARRY ON THE REVOLUTION – IN **PAUL GOODMAN'S** PHRASE, "TO CREATE AR-EAS OF FREEDOM" – EACH IN OUR **OWN** WAY. THE REPORTER SHOOK HER HEAD AND **LEFT** THE ROOM BEFORE WE DID.

THE REST OF THE SORRY WAR, THE EXILES, THE DEPARTURES AND BREAKUPS ALL **WAITED** FOR US, AND A GLOOM **DESCENDED** THAT IS ONLY **NOW** BEGINNING TO LIFT.

END

Near the end of the 1960's, and
quite unanticipated by SDS leaders,
high schoolers began coming to
demonstrations and then actually
chartering SDS chapters.

A Children's Revolution by James D. Cennamo

DURING THE 1960's, I LIVED IN BROOKLYN, NEW YORK. OUR NEIGHBORHOOD WAS MADE UP OF ITALIAN, IRISH, AND JEWISH AMERICANS.

MY BEST FRIEND WAS JEWISH. HIS DAD TAUGHT COLLEGE AND HIS MOM WAS A SOCIAL WORKER. I LIKED THEM A LOT.

SOMETIMES THEY WOULD GET TOGETHER AND SING SONGS FROM A MAGAZINE CALLED "SING OUT."

I WANTED DESPERATELY TO BECOME A **JEW!**

IN 1967 MY FRIEND DAVID AND I TURNED 13.

THE WAR IN VIETNAM WAS RAGING AND THE COUNTER-CULTURE WAS SEEPING INTO OUR CONSCIOUSNESS...

WE HEARD ABOUT **SDS.** I THOUGHT THE NAME SOUNDED SINISTER.

IT'S STUDENTS FOR A DEMOCRATIC SOCIETY.

OH, THAT SOUNDS GOOD!

WE WERE TOO YOUNG TO JOIN, SO WE SATISFIED OURSELVES BY EMULATING THEM.

LOOK WHAT I DID!

NEAT! LOOK AT MINE.

BRING THE WAR HOME

STUDENT POWER

WE MADE T-SHIRTS AND SCRAWLED SLOGANS WITH CHALK ON THE STREET.

THE TIME HAD COME FOR US TO ORGANIZE OUR OWN GROUP.

DAVID'S SIBLINGS: DANNY 'N RACHEL.

JODY FELDMAN, A GIRL I WAS IN LOVE WITH!

WE NEEDED A NAME FOR OUR GROUP. WE HAD MANY IDEAS...

THE KIDS REVOLUTIONARY GUARD!?

THE LITTLE PEACE-NIKS.

DR. SPOCK'S KIDS.

IT WAS SETTLED. WE WOULD BE KNOWN AS...

C.S.P.
CHILDREN'S STRIKE FOR PEACE

WE PUBLISHED A NEWSLETTER AND SENT IT TO FRIENDS.

How DO YOU SPELL "IMPERIALISM"?

WHAT'S IMPERIALISM?

CLACK CLACK

OUR SHINING MOMENT: WE WERE GRANTED A POSITION IN THE APRIL **PEACE MARCH** IN NYC. WE MARCHED FROM CENTRAL PARK TO THE U.N.

WE WERE VERY PROUD THAT DAY. WE WONDERED IF WE MADE A DIFFERENCE.

AFTER A WHILE OUR GROUP FIZZLED OUT. THE WAR CONTINUED AND ATROCITIES WERE EXPOSED DAILY.

THE WAR WAS OVER! DAVID BECAME A LAWYER IN THE 80's; DANNY, A SOCIAL WORKER... RACHEL, A TEACHER. I DON'T KNOW WHAT BECAME OF JODY.

MY FAMILY MOVED TO BOSTON IN '69. I NEVER DID BECOME JEWISH, BUT I DO FOLLOW A SPIRITUAL PATH. I PRAY FOR ALL WARS TO END. I PRAY FOR PEACE BECAUSE IT MAKES ME FEEL LIKE A **BOY AGAIN**, BACK IN '67 – BROOKLYN, N.Y.

'06 Cennamo

James D. Cennamo, namojames@yahoo.com

END

175

National officers made a particular
point of confronting meetings of
local chapters within easy driving
range with demands for factional
support.

TURN YOUR CHAIRS AROUND

STORY BY MAX ELBAUM & HARVEY PEKAR   ART BY GARY DUMM

I WAS PART OF THE **LEADERSHIP** TEAM PLANNING THE **FIRST SDS** MEETING OF THE **NEW** SEMESTER AT THE U OF WISCONSIN, MADISON. WE WERE EXPECTING A **BIG** TURNOUT. MANY **STUDENTS** BEYOND THE **300-STRONG** SDS CORE WERE **EAGER** TO FIND OUT PLANS FOR A BIG **FALL** MOBILIZATION. THEY ALSO KNEW THAT **SDS** ON A **NATIONAL** LEVEL HAD SPLIT AND EXPLODED AT ITS **JUNE 1969 CONVENTION** AND WANTED TO HEAR WHAT THE **MADISON SDS** ACTIVISTS HAD TO SAY ABOUT THIS "BIG BANG."

THE LEADERSHIP **GROUP** OF **10 - 15** WAS **EXCITED.** WE WEREN'T FOCUSED ON GETTING **MADISON ACTIVISTS** TO LINE UP BEHIND ONE OR ANOTHER **SIDE** IN THE NATIONWIDE **FACTION** FIGHT. WE WERE **MORE** INTERESTED IN BUILDING ON THE POLITICAL **MOMENTUM** OF THE **PREVIOUS** YEAR TO WAGE AN AGGRESSIVE **CAMPAIGN** ON CAMPUS, ESPECIALLY AGAINST THE **VIETNAM WAR** AND THE **UNIVERSITY OF WISCONSIN'S COMPLICITY** WITH IT.

ONE THING **WORRIED** US. WE HAD HEARD **RUMORS** THAT A **CREW** FROM ONE OF THE NATIONAL **SDS** FACTIONS, THE **WEATHERMEN**, WAS HEADED TO **MADISON** FROM **CHICAGO**, TRYING TO **WIN** SUPPORT FOR THEIR UPCOMING **DAYS OF RAGE** NATIONAL **ACTION.**

BAP!

THE **LAST** THING WE WANTED TO **HAPPEN** WAS A **BRAWL** AMONG **RADICALS** WITH THE **CHANCE** THAT RADICALISM'S BASE COULD BE REDUCED DRAMATICALLY RIGHT IN **FRONT** OF US. THE **PUBLICITY** WOULDN'T BE GOOD.

IT WAS **AGREED** THAT I WAS **CAPABLE** OF **STICKING** TO THE APPROVED **GUIDELINES** AND KEEPING **COOL**, SO I WAS PICKED TO **CHAIR** THE MEETING.

THE MEETING **CONVENED** IN THE GREAT HALL OF THE **UNIVERSITY** OF **WISCONSIN'S STUDENT UNION** ONE EVENING DURING THE **FIRST WEEK** OF THE NEW SEMESTER. THERE WAS A CROWD OF **500+** BY THE APPOINTED HOUR. IN ONE OF THE MOST **ONTIME** BEGINNINGS OF ANY **SDS** MEETING, WE TURNED ON THE SOUND SYSTEM AND **STARTED OFF** RIGHT AS PLANNED. IN **NO TIME** WE WERE MOVING INTO A SERIES OF **PRESENTATIONS** ON VARIOUS **ORGANIZING** IDEAS FOR THE **NEXT YEAR.**

THEN, **TWENTY MINUTES** INTO THE SESSION, A LINE OF A **DOZEN PEOPLE** ENTERED THE ROOM FROM THE BACK. THEY **BRUSHED** ASIDE REQUESTS TO TAKE **SEATS** AND WALKED DOWN THE **LEFT** SIDE OF THE HALL, AND **CLIMBED** THE STEPS TO THE **STAGE.** THESE **WEATHERMEN** WOULD **NOT** SIT IN THE AUDIENCE, WHICH WAS GETTING **STIRRED UP** TOO. SO I FOLLOWED THE **COURSE** AGREED UPON, **HOPPED** DOWN FROM THE **STAGE,** AND LOUDLY SAID THAT THE LEADERSHIP WAS **ASKING** EVERYONE TO **STAY CALM.**

EVERYONE TAKE IT **EASY**...DON'T DO ANYTHING **FOOLISH.**

A WEATHERPERSON TOOK THE **MICROPHONE** AND BEGAN TO **HARANGUE** THE CROWD. HE SAID THEY WANTED TO "**BRING THE WAR HOME,**" AND THAT THE **NEXT** STEP WAS A **DAYS OF RAGE** RALLY SET FOR **OCTOBER** IN CHICAGO...

ANYONE WHO DOESN'T GO IS A **WIMP!**

SOON FOLKS BEGAN TO **HECKLE** AND DEMAND AND EVEN **THREATEN** THE **WEATHERMEN**, WHO WOULD NOT **LEAVE**. **SUDDENLY** THE MIC IN THE **WEATHERMAN'S** HANDS WENT **DEAD**.

BOOO!

SIT DOWN!

FROM **ANOTHER** MIC IN THE **BACK** OF THE ROOM WAS HEARD...

OKAY EVERYBODY, WE'VE ALL HAD **ENOUGH** OF THIS. **TURN** YOUR **CHAIRS** AROUND AND WE'LL **CONTINUE** THE **MEETING**.

THERE WAS **THIRTY SECONDS** OF **NOISE** AS PEOPLE **MOVED** THEIR **CHAIRS**, THEN THE **NEXT** SPEAKER WAS **INTRODUCED**.

BACK ON STAGE THE **WEATHERMEN** WERE CAUGHT **OFF GUARD**. NO ONE TURNED TO **LISTEN** TO WHAT THEY WERE **SAYING**. THE **WEATHERMEN** WERE MORE **LAUGHABLE** THAN INTIMIDATING.

I MET ONE OF THE DOZEN **WEATHERMEN** LATER...HE WAS A **UW** STUDENT, AND AFTER A FEW **MORE** WEEKS HE **QUIT** THE **WEATHERMEN** AND CAME BACK TO **MADISON**. WE HAD A GOOD **LAUGH** ABOUT THE **WHOLE** THING.

YEAH... Y'KNOW?!

HAR-DE-HAR-HAR!

END

179

The crack-up of SDS left behind
shards of activism and a deep
sense of personal disorientation.
The women's movement, the gay and
lesbian movement, and the Chicano
movement were just beginning.

AUSTIN STORIES PART 2

STORY BY MARIANN WIZARD WITH ALICE EMBREE AND HARVEY PEKAR   ART BY GARY DUMM

FALL 1969

Things are changing FAST now. The ANTIWAR movement is HUGE but SDS has come apart at the SEAMS, and the WAR is still GROWING. PROGRESSIVE LABOR and "ANTI-PL" forces such as the REVOLUTIONARY YOUTH MOVEMENT, which mirrors PL'S TACTICS, DOMINATED SDS MEETINGS DURING THE PREVIOUS YEAR.

SDS

But over the SUMMER, Austin SDSers and others traveled the STATE'S small campuses, spreading the RADICAL word. Did we need ANOTHER faction? AUSTIN SDS, like other "PROVINCIAL" chapters, DISASSOCIATES FROM BOTH NATIONAL OFFICES. SDS NOW is less an ORGANIZATION than INTERRELATED GROUPS OF FRIENDS who SHARE A COMMON HISTORY, and TOLERATE, WHILE OFTEN ARGUING, EACH OTHER'S OPINION. NO ONE KNOWS WHAT THE CORRECT "LINE" IS ANYMORE; AT LEAST THAT MUCH SEEMS SETTLED.

AT THE UT STUDENT UNION...

DID YOU HEAR WHAT HAPPENED TO DICK?

NO, WHAT? DID A BUS HIT HIM, I HOPE, THE STUBBORN SON OF A BITCH!

HE'S BEEN EXPELLED FROM PROGRESSIVE LABOR AND BECKY'S DIVORCING HIM.

SHIT, THE POOR BASTARD! WHAT HAPPENED?

HE WAS INVOLVED WITH SOMEONE FROM ANOTHER FACTION. SOMEBODY FOUND OUT. THEY TRIED HIM AS A COUNTER-REVOLUTIONARY, AND HE'S OUT. BECKY'S GOING TO THE NATIONAL OFFICE OF PL-SDS.

GREAT. PL STICKS ITS NOSE INTO THE BEDROOM. THAT'S SURE TO BE POPULAR WITH THE WORKING CLASS. HOW'S DICK TAKING IT?

PRETTY BAD. WE HEARD THAT CAT'S BEEN PL'S TRUE BELIEVER HERE. AND NOW IT'S LIKE HE'S EXCOMMUNICATED OR IS A LEPER, YA KNOW?

I'M SORRY FOR BECKY. SHE'S ALWAYS BEEN TOTALLY DEVOTED TO HIM.

SHE'LL GET OVER IT.

181

TREES ARE BULLDOZED ON CAMPUS DESPITE STUDENTS' PROTEST.

A COFFEEHOUSE BECOMES A CENTER OF **DRAFT** AND **WAR** **RESISTANCE. GI'S** AND **VETS** OFTEN COME IN.

I'LL LET YOU KNOW HOW IT IS IN CANADA. MAN, I AIN'T GOING BACK TO DA NANG.

VAYA BIEN, HERMANO!

SO I'VE BEEN **DRAFTED** OUT OF **GRADUATE** SCHOOL. I'LL BE IN THE **ARMY** NEXT WEEK. I DON'T KNOW WHERE THEY'LL **SEND** ME, BUT I'M GONNA **ORGANIZE** WHEREVER I AM.

IT'S NOT JUST VIETNAM...WE'VE GOT TO SET IN MOTION A **PROCESS** THAT WILL ALSO STOP THE **SEVENTH** WAR FROM NOW.

SHIT...IF MORE PEOPLE **KNEW** WHAT WAS GOING ON IN 'NAM – CATS **REFUSING** ORDERS AND **TAKING** OUT OFFICERS WHO ARE TOO **"GUNG-HO"** – THEY'D MAYBE BE A LOT MORE **MILITANT! GI'S** WANT THIS **WAR** OVER **NOW.**

NOVEMBER 1969: THE POLICE **ATTACK** STUDENT **REVOLUTIONARIES** AT THE CHUCK WAGON, AN **EATERY** IN THE STUDENT UNION.

IN MARCH 1970 A BLAST IN A NEW YORK CITY APARTMENT HOUSE KILLS SDS MEMBERS TERRY ROBBINS, DIANA OUGHTON, AND TED GOLD. THE "PORT HURON"-STYLE SDS IS GONE AS THE WEATHER UNDERGROUND EMERGES.

FORMER AUSTIN SDSER MARILYN BUCK ATTENDS A RALLY IN SAN FRANCISCO.

APRIL 1970: AUSTIN'S JEFF JONES IS ELECTED THE **FIRST** AVOWEDLY **RADICAL** STUDENT BODY **PRESIDENT.**

THE GRADUATE STUDENT VOTE PUT US OVER THE TOP... WE'VE WON!

MAY 4: AUSTIN STUDENTS **STRIKE** ON BEHALF OF KENT **STATE** STUDENTS. A **HUGE MASS** OF STUDENTS **ATTEMPT,** LED BY **JONES,** TO MARCH DOWNTOWN BUT ARE **STOPPED** BY POLICE **TEAR GAS.**

RELAXING ON AN SDS MEMBER'S PORCH AFTER THE CONFRONTATION...

ANYBODY WANT ANY FRUIT PUNCH? IT'S GOT "ACID" IN IT.

LATER, BACK AT THE THREATENED PARK...

WHANG!

WHANG! WANG! WHANG! WHANG!

WELL, SO MUCH FOR ALICE BEING RESERVED.

185

MARIANN AND ALICE ARE DRINKING COFFEE AND MAKING DECISIONS.

IT'S ALL FALLING APART.

IT'S A CULTURE OF VIOLENCE.

AL, I'M LEAVING AUSTIN. I'M GONNA MEET LARRY AT FORT ORD. HE'S HELPING ORGANIZE GI'S AGAINST THE WAR THERE. I CAN'T BE A STUDENT ANYMORE. AND PETE, THEY KILLED PART OF HIM IN 'NAM AND HE'S TOO DAMNED DUTCH TO LAY DOWN. I'VE GOT TO KEEP TRYING TO STOP THIS WAR EVEN IF SDS IS OVER.

I KNOW...ME TOO. I CAN'T FACE SEEING EVERYTHING I GREW UP LOVING DESTROYED RIGHT IN FRONT OF ME. I'M JOINING SOME WOMEN, MIDWIVES ON A FARM IN ARKANSAS, TO TRY TO MAKE A SAFE PLACE FOR PEOPLE...TRY TO SURVIVE WHAT'S COMING.

ARE YOU SURE YOU WANT TO HOOK UP WITH ANOTHER MAN, MAR?

I DON'T THINK WE CAN MAKE A REVOLUTION WITHOUT 'EM...AND WE DON'T NEED MIDWIVES WITHOUT 'EM EITHER.

186

WE'LL MEET AGAIN, SIS.

-END

WITH SDSER MICHAEL BALTER AT UCLA AND IN THE ARMY

STORY BY
MICHAEL BALTER & HARVEY PEKAR

ART BY GARY DUMM

THEY WERE **FRIENDS** OF MY GIRLFRIEND, **FERN.** THE WAY THEY GOT ME **INVOLVED...SDS** PUT OUT A **NEWSLETTER** CALLED **"THE AARDVARK."** THE PERSON WHO STARTED AND WAS **EDITING** IT NO LONGER WANTED TO **DO** IT. THEY NEEDED A **NEW** EDITOR, SO THEY CAME TO **ME** AND SAID, "WOULD YOU LIKE TO TAKE ON THIS **PROJECT?**" I THOUGHT IT WOULD BE PRETTY **EXCITING** TO DO, SORT OF LIKE AN **OPEN** FIELD.

SDS WAS A PRETTY **SECTARIAN** THING AT UCLA. IT WASN'T LONG BEFORE THE PL PEOPLE IN **SDS** TOOK ME **UNDER** THEIR WING AND I BEGAN TO GET MY POLITICAL **EDUCATION.** AT THE BEGINNING OF **1969, SDS** ON CAMPUS BEGAN A CAMPAIGN AROUND **OPEN ADMISSION** TO MINORITIES. IT WAS IN **RESPONSE** TO THE **SAN FRANCISCO STATE** STRIKE.

WE PUT FORWARD **PETITIONS** — WE WERE REALLY ADVOCATING **OPEN ADMISSIONS** — TO LET **ALL MINORITY** HIGH SCHOOL **GRADUATES** WHO WANTED TO COME TO **UCLA** COME. RIGHT ABOUT THAT TIME THE **BLACK STUDENT** MOVEMENT AT **UCLA** BECAME VERY **STRONG.** **WHITE** STUDENTS BY THE **THOUSANDS** WERE **FLOCKING** TO CLASSES BASED ON **"THE AUTOBIOGRAPHY OF MALCOLM X."**

187

WE HAD AN ILLEGAL RALLY. **THREE LAPD** PLAIN-CLOTHES OFFICERS, WHO SOMEBODY **RECOGNIZED**, WERE IN THE CROWD. POLICE ON CAMPUS WAS A **BIG** ISSUE. WE **CHASED** THEM OFF. WE LITERALLY **ESCORTED** THEM OFF CAMPUS. THEY WERE **WALKING** AND WE WERE **BEHIND** THEM, GETTING THEM TO **MOVE** IN A **FORWARD** DIRECTION.

THE NEXT QUARTER STARTED, AND THEY WERE WITHOLDING MY REGISTRATION PACKET ON **SEVERAL** GROUNDS. THERE WAS A PENDING **DISCIPLINARY** PROCEEDING AGAINST ME FOR **ILLEGAL** USE OF THE SOUND SYSTEM AND HAVING AN ILLEGAL **RALLY**. I WAS THE **MAIN** SPEAKER AT THIS RALLY.

THERE WAS A **TAKEOVER** OF THE ADMINISTRATION BUILDING. THE **FACULTY CENTER** WAS SURROUNDED, AND **GOVERNOR REAGAN** COULD NOT **GET OUT**. CHANCELLOR **YOUNG'S** PROMISE **NOT** TO BRING POLICE ON CAMPUS WAS **BROKEN**. THE TV CAMERA SHOWED **REAGAN** COMING OUT OF THE **FRONT** DOOR OF THE FACULTY CENTER **SMILING** AND **WAVING**.

THE CAMERA DID **NOT** SHOW THAT A **HUNDRED** FEET AWAY WERE **THREE THOUSAND** PEOPLE. THAT WAS THE **MOST** MILITANT **DEMONSTRATION** I **EVER** SAW AT UCLA.

THEN I WENT **INTO** THE **ARMY. BASIC** TRAINING WAS SUCH A **HARASSING** AND **INTIMIDATING** TIME THAT I DIDN'T DO MUCH. I DID PASS OUT SOME **LEAFLETS**. THERE WERE A NUMBER OF OTHER PL – SDSERS THERE BECAUSE **EVERYONE** WENT TO **FORT ORD** FOR **BASIC** TRAINING.

EVERYBODY **HATED** THE ARMY, NOBODY **REALLY UNDERSTOOD** WHAT THE **WAR** WAS ALL ABOUT, AND PEOPLE WERE **VERY RECEPTIVE.** I WAS SURPRISED. WHAT WE DID MOST **SUCCESSFULLY** WAS **ORGANIZING** AROUND **ISSUES** AT THE FORT.

BLACK AND **LATINO GI'S, ESPECIALLY BLACK** GI'S, WERE ALWAYS RUNNING **AFOUL** OF DRILL SERGEANTS AND THE **BRASS,** ALWAYS COMING IN FOR **EXTRA HARASSMENT.** THERE WAS **SELECTIVE COURT-MARTIALING** AND THINGS LIKE THAT. WE FORMED **DEFENSE COMMITTEES** TO **ATTEND** COURTS-MARTIAL OF ALMOST EXCLUSIVELY **BLACK** GI'S. WE USED TO SAY "**MILITARY JUSTICE** IS TO JUSTICE WHAT **MILITARY MUSIC** IS TO MUSIC."

MY FAVORITE THING WAS IN 1970. **CESAR CHAVEZ** WAS ORGANIZING A LETTUCE **STRIKE** 15 MILES FROM **SALINAS. FORT ORD,** WITH **30,000** GI'S, WAS THE **LARGEST** BUYER OF SALINAS VALLEY LETTUCE. SO WE BEGAN A LETTUCE **BOYCOTT,** MY ROOMMATE AND I. WE DID THIS **SPONTANEOUSLY**...AND WE TOOK GI'S DOWN TO THE **PICKET LINES.**

BOYCOTT LETTUCE

I HAD **TWO** COURTS-MARTIAL, AND I WAS CHARGED **FIVE TIMES**...ONE WAS A **SUMMARY COURT-MARTIAL.** USUALLY IT WAS FOR **DISTRIBUTING LITERATURE** OR BEING **AWOL.** THE MOST **IMPORTANT** COURT-MARTIAL WAS AFTER THE INVASION OF **CAMBODIA** IN **MAY 1970.** WE JOINED THE DEMONSTRATORS ON **HIGHWAY ONE.**

LATER THEY GOT **RID** OF US **ALL.** WE BEGAN TO HAVE DEMONSTRATIONS ON **FISHERMAN'S WHARF** IN **MONTEREY** IN **UNIFORM.** THEY COULD HAVE **PUT** ME IN THE **STOCKADE,** BUT THEY **DIDN'T** WANT ME **THERE,** EITHER. THEY WERE **DEALING** WITH A PRETTY **DISAFFECTED** BUNCH OF **SOLDIERS.**

END **189**

THE NEW LEFT, **WITHOUT** OFFICIAL SDS PARTICIPATION CONTINUED THEIR FIGHT -- WHICH CAME TO AN AWFUL, BLOODY CLIMAX ON MAY 4TH, 1970.

WHAT CAN WE DO NOW?

RICHARD NIXON HAD ANNOUNCED ON APRIL 30 THAT HE WAS, IN EFFECT, VIOLATING HIS OWN POLICIES AS WELL AS **INTERNATIONAL LAW** BY SECRETLY DIRECTING AMERICAN TROOPS TO **INVADE CAMBODIA.**

IMMEDIATELY, THERE WERE DEMONSTRATIONS AND PROTESTS ON COLLEGE CAMPUSES **ALL OVER** THE U.S.

SEVERAL DAYS LATER AT KENT STATE, THE **OHIO NATIONAL GUARD** FIRED 67 SHOTS IN 13 SECONDS AT A DEFENSELESS GROUP OF STUDENT PROTESTERS. **FOUR WERE KILLED INSTANTLY AND NINE WOUNDED.** THE GUARD'S ACTION HAD BEEN COMPLETELY **UNPROVOKED.**

IN THE AFTERMATH, **NO ACTION** WAS TAKEN AGAINST THE TROOPS BY A COUNTY GRAND JURY. IT APPARENTLY WAS **OPEN SEASON** ON STUDENT PROTESTERS!

THE KILLINGS OF STUDENTS AT KENT STATE AND ALSO JACKSON STATE TURNED THE TIDE IN MUCH PUBLIC SENTIMENT, COMPELLING MANY LIBERALS, UNIVERSITY OFFICIALS, AND EVEN BLUE-COLLAR WORKERS TO **OPPOSE** CONTINUED U.S. OCCUPATION OF VIETNAM. STILL, THERE WAS A **CRACKDOWN** ALL OVER THE COUNTRY ON POLITICAL PROTEST, AND WE DIDN'T GET OUT OF VIETNAM UNTIL **1975.**

PEACENIKS WERE CERTAIN, **ESPECIALLY** AFTER THE '72 PRESIDENTIAL ELECTION, THAT MOST OF THE OVER-30 POPULATION WAS **OUT OF THEIR MINDS** FOR SUPPORTING NIXON -- THE **SAME MAN** THEY DROPPED LIKE A BAD HABIT WHEN **WATERGATE** BEGAN MAKING HEADLINES.

DUH.

AND THINGS HAVE GOTTEN WORSE. NOW WE'RE BOGGED DOWN IN **ANOTHER** QUAGMIRE IN IRAQ. PLUS THE WORLD FACES A LOOMING DISASTER DUE TO GLOBAL WARMING, AND THE AVERAGE U.S. CITIZEN HAS **NO IDEA** WHAT THAT MEANS.

LIKE I ALWAYS SAY: AVERAGE IS DUMB.

END
FEB 2007

WEATHERMEN

WASHINGTON, D.C. – NOVEMBER 15, 1969

BY WES MODES

MONTHS AFTER THE **DAYS OF RAGE**, THE WEATHERMEN TOOK PART IN A DEMONSTRATION IN WASHINGTON, D.C. THIS WAS A BIG ANTIWAR DEMONSTRATION THAT WAS INTENDED AS A **MORE MILITANT** VERSION OF THE SUCCESSFUL NATIONWIDE DEMOS THAT HAD HAPPENED A **MONTH EARLIER**.

I WAS PART OF THE **WEATHERMEN** (SOON TO BECOME THE **WEATHER UNDERGROUND**) AND HAD FOUGHT COPS IN THE STREETS OF CHICAGO IN JUNE. I WAS **WEEKS** AWAY FROM GOING UNDERGROUND MYSELF. I ALREADY HAD A FALSE ID AND A SAFE HOUSE AND A ROUTE PLANNED TO **CANADA**.

HALF A MILLION ANGRY PEOPLE!

THE WEATHERMEN SPONSORED SEVERAL ACTIONS INCLUDING AN ATTACK ON THE JUSTICE DEPARTMENT! DURING THE DEMONSTRATION, WE **BROKE OFF** FROM THE MAIN MARCH.

WE WERE EQUIPPED WITH **HELMETS, GOGGLES,** AND **GAS MASKS.** WE HANDED OUT **STUFF TO THROW** — BASEBALLS, BRICKS, STONES. I HAD BOTTLES OF **RED INK!**

TO THE INJUSTICE BUILDING!

Air

FOR THE BLOOD OF OUR NLF COMPATRIOTS!

WE WERE CONCERNED THERE MIGHT BE SNIPERS ON THE ROOF! WE LOOKED UP AND WE COULD SEE ATTORNEY GENERAL JOHN MITCHELL WATCHING US!

THE STREETS WERE **PACKED!** THERE WERE THOUSANDS OF PEOPLE. AND THEY WERE **ANGRY** ABOUT VIETNAM. THE FEELING WAS THAT WE WERE GOING TO **WAR!**

HANDS OFF

FUCK YOU!

GET OUT

POLICE ON **HORSEBACK** CHARGED THE CROWD. FROM THE OTHER SIDE POLICE LINES MARCHED FORWARD! FROM A GARAGE ACROSS THE STREET, **NATIONAL GUARD SOLDIERS** IN TRUCKS DROVE RIGHT INTO THE MELEE! PEOPLE WERE SO MAD THEY **STOOD THEIR GROUND!** PLUS THERE WAS **NOWHERE TO GO!**

I'VE NEVER SEEN STREET FIGHTING LIKE IT. PEOPLE WERE GETTING HURT, ARRESTED! THE **PIGS** WERE FIGHTING WITH GAS, BATONS, AND HORSES! PEOPLE WERE FIGHTING WITH WHATEVER THEY COULD GET THEIR **HANDS ON!** IT WENT ON **FOREVER.** WHEN WE TOOK OFF, THE JUSTICE BUILDING WAS **TRASHED.**

—END

"IT WAS JUST **PURE INSANITY**... FROM THE STANDPOINT OF RATIONAL POLITICS AND ORGANIZATION WE WERE **OUT OF OUR MINDS.** ON THE **OTHER** HAND, AS A RESPONSE TO WHAT WAS GOING ON IN **VIETNAM**, IT WAS A RESPONSE OF **TOTAL OUTRAGE**... AT THE TIME IT DIDN'T SEEM LIKE WE WERE HAVING ANY IMPACT AT **ALL**, AND IT WAS A GESTURE OF **TOTAL FRUSTRATION**, WHICH WAS TO GO **BANANAS**, AND AS SUCH WAS A VERY **SANE** RESPONSE. SO EVEN THOUGH IT WAS **TOTALLY CRAZY** AS A POLITICAL ACT, HISTORY CAN'T, DOESN'T, HASN'T CONDEMNED IT."
—CATHY WILKERSON
WEATHER UNDERGROUND

Housed in the State Historical Society of Wisconsin's Social Movement Collection were civil rights and labor materials that had been gathered for more than a decade, as well as one of the most thorough collections of labor and radical newspapers anywere.

195

196

ADVENTURES IN

PARTICIPATORY

DEMOCRACY

In 1965 I left **WISCONSIN** and came to a women's college in **MASSACHUSETTS**. I was eager to **LEARN**.

Becoming **UPSET** about the war in **VIETNAM**, I joined the local **PEACE VIGIL**.

Ever **CURIOUS**, I went to an **SDS** meeting at a nearby **MEN'S** college.

A woman in **SDS** gave me some **LITERATURE** to read...

FREEDOM OF SPEECH

PARTICIPATORY DEMOCRACY

SDS

PORT HURON STATEMENT

YES!

CIVIL RIGHTS

JUSTICE

VIET NAM

Back at my **DORM** I talked to all my friends about **SDS** and the **WAR**.

197

I BEGAN GOING TO **SDS** MEETINGS REGULARLY. LISTENING AND WATCHING **CLOSELY,** I TRIED TO UNDERSTAND BUT NEVER FELT KNOWLEDGEABLE **ENOUGH** TO VOLUNTEER FOR ANYTHING.

YADDA-TALK-TALK YADDA-TALK-TALK YADDA!

HMMM?

THEN ONE DAY AT AN **SDS** MEETING THE CHAIRMAN SAID:

NOBODY WILL **VOLUNTEER** TO **WORK** ON OUR **INTERNAL EDUCATION PROJECT.**

IF YOU WANT SOMETHING TO GET **DONE,** DON'T **ASK** FOR **VOLUNTEERS.** JUST **POINT** TO ONE AND SAY **"WILL YOU DO IT?"**

THE FINGER POINTED AT ME.

WILL YOU HELP?

PARTICIPATORY DEMOCRACY MEANS BEING WILLING TO **ACTIVELY** PARTICIPATE. WHAT COULD I **SAY?**

YIKES!

OKAY – BUT I DON'T **EVEN** KNOW WHAT **INTERNAL EDUCATION** MEANS.

THAT'S OKAY – I'LL HELP YOU.

RISING TO MEET THE **CHALLENGE**, I LEARNED A **LOT**, FAST.

GET SPEAKER ✓
BOOK ROOM ✓
MAKE POSTERS

MAKING **POSTERS** ON AN OLD HANDSET PLATEN **PRESS** WAS **CREATIVE**, MESSY, AND **FUN**.

SDS

DISTRIBUTING THEM **WASN'T**. IT WAS A TIME-CONSUMING **CHORE**, SO I DID ONLY MY CAMPUS AND LEFT OTHER POSTERS FOR THE **CHAIRMAN** OF **SDS** TO PUT UP AT **HIS** CAMPUS.

SDS

NEXT YEAR **SDS** HAD A **NEW** CHAIRMAN.

I HAVE TO **STUDY** – **COULD** YOU POSTER **HERE**, TOO?

OKAY.

SOMEONE HAS TO DO IT... HOW CAN I SAY **NO?**

AND SO, WHEN THE CHAIRMAN NEXT ASKED...

SANDY, WILL *YOU* CHAIR THE MEETING TONIGHT?

HE WANTS ME TO HELP HIM LOOK GOOD TO THE REGIONAL REP – BUT I DON'T HAVE TO DO WHATEVER HE WANTS.

NO!

I GUESS SHE DOESN'T WANT ME TO LIBERATE HER.

FREEDOM

I BEGAN SILENTLY **COUNTING** THE NUMBER OF MALES AND FEMALES AT OUR **MEETINGS**... **WHO WAS TALKING**, WHO CARRIED **DECISIONS**, AND WHO DID THE **SHIT-WORK**.

I WASN'T THE ONLY WOMAN WHO DID THIS.

WOMEN IN OUR **SDS** CHAPTER BEGAN ORGANIZING DEMONSTRATIONS AT **OUR** CAMPUS. BUT ONLY A **FEW** GUYS CAME.

201

WE WOMEN BEGAN MEETING BY OURSELVES AND DECIDED TO HAVE OUR OWN SDS CHAPTER AT OUR CAMPUS. WE STILL SUPPORTED ACTIONS AT THE MEN'S CAMPUS — BUT THEY DID THEIR OWN POSTERING.

MOST OF THE GUYS UNDERSTOOD, BUT SOME DIDN'T.

SANDY, CAN YOU SEW THE BANNER FOR US?

I THINK YOU SHOULD SEW IT YOURSELF!

YOU'VE GOT A REAL PROBLEM!

HOW CAN YOU WASTE TIME ON PERSONAL ISSUES WHEN THERE'S A WAR GOING ON?

BUT WHAT DOES PARTICIPATORY DEMOCRACY REALLY MEAN? AND WHAT ARE THE ISSUES THAT AFFECT OUR LIVES AS WOMEN?

EMPOWERMENT

NO!

YES!

WOMEN'S LIBERATION

EQUAL PAY FOR EQUAL WORK

REPRODUCTIVE RIGHTS

I DON'T HAVE TO OBEY MEN

I DESERVE RESPECT

AS WOMEN WE DECIDED TO SPEAK TO OTHER WOMEN ON WOMEN'S ISSUES.

202

THE DISCUSSION ENTERED DORMS AND CLASSROOMS, SPREADING ACROSS CAMPUS...

DRESS CODES.

WHAT DO WE WANT FOR OURSELVES?

CAREER OR MARRIAGE?

SISTERHOOD IS POWERFUL.

...AND 25 YEARS LATER WHEN MY CLASSMATES WERE POLLED ON WHICH POLITICAL MOVEMENT HAD THE GREATEST IMPACT ON THEIR LIVES, THE ANSWER WAS:

☐ CIVIL RIGHTS

☑ WOMEN'S LIBERAT

☐ ANTIWAR

LESSONS IN PARTICIPATORY DEMOCRACY...

* Participate but don't try to do everything yourself. Spread the tasks so everyone can participate.

* Be democratic. Encourage everyone to speak. Listen to each other and cooperate. Seek consensus rather than dominance.

* Working together, we can make a difference.

END

In the decades following the 1960's the demography of American youth shifted dramatically, and a new generation of students, more insecure, much more often the children of immigrants, arrived.

I'M BRUCE RUBENSTEIN. I WAS IN SDS FROM 1966 ON. I ATTENDED THE LAST SDS CONVENTION AND LATER WAS IN THE WEATHER ORGANIZATION.

THE WEATHERMEN ARE GONE BUT SDS IS BACK, NOW AS STRONG AS IT WAS IN 1966, AMONG STUDENTS AND OTHERS IN A WORLD THAT NEEDS IT MORE THAN EVER.

SDS REVIVED

Story by
BRUCE RUBENSTEIN
&
PAUL BUHLE
Art by ED PISKOR

SDS OF THE 1960'S IS REMEMBERED FOR ITS AGGRESSIVE COUNTERATTACK AGAINST THE WAR MACHINE INVADING THE CAMPUS, TURNING ACADEMIES OF KNOWLEDGE INTO ACCESSORIES TO MASS MURDER.

AND IT IS REMEMBERED, AFTER THE SDS COLLAPSE, FOR THE GROUP CALLING ITSELF WEATHERMEN, TAKEN FROM A BOB DYLAN SONG.

BUT SDS OF THE 1960'S **SHOULD** BE REMEMBERED FOR ITS UNIQUE DECENTRALIZED DEMOCRACY, WITH STUDENTS DECIDING ON EACH CAMPUS WHAT THEY NEEDED TO DO. THEY CALLED IT STUDENT SYNDICALISM.

SDS WAS STARTED UP AGAIN ON MARTIN LUTHER KING, JR., HOLIDAY OF 2006. ITS TWO FOUNDERS WERE THE FIRST PRESIDENT OF SDS, AL HABER, AND CONNECTICUT HIGH SCHOOL SENIOR PAT KORTE.

RAPIDLY, THE WORD SPREAD AMONG HUNDREDS OF YOUNG PEOPLE ACROSS THE COUNTRY: SDS IS BACK.

LONGTIME NEXTLEFTNOTES.NET EDITOR TOM GOOD WAS BUILDING AN ONLINE NETWORK CONNECTING EXISTING CHAPTERS, HELPING START MANY NEW CHAPTERS, AND TELLING JOKES.

AN APRIL REGIONAL CONFERENCE IN PROVIDENCE, RHODE ISLAND, AND AN AUGUST NATIONAL CONFERENCE IN CHICAGO BROUGHT ACTIVISTS TOGETHER.

BY THE FALL, SDS WAS ORGANIZING A MOVEMENT FOR A DEMOCRATIC SOCIETY (MDS). OLDER RADICALS, INCLUDING 1960'S SDSERS, WILL ASSIST STUDENTS AND HELP SET OUT A COMPREHENSIVE PROGRAM OF ACTIVITIES ON CAMPUS AND OFF, AND RECRUIT ACTIVISTS IN THEIR OWN RIGHT.

OUTMODED THEORIES, STRATEGIES, AND TACTICS LIKE VANGUARD PARTIES AND THE DICTATORSHIP OF THE PROLETARIAT HAVE BEEN REPLACED BY ORGANIZING AROUND A SET OF NEW IDEAS DEVISED FOR THE TWENTY-FIRST CENTURY.

THIS IS THE FIRST MULTI-GENERATIONAL, DIVERSE RADICAL MOVEMENT WITH EVERYONE AS AN EQUAL PARTICIPANT.

END

ACKNOWLEDGMENTS

Two strips utilize materials from the Oral History Office of Columbia University, and we are happy to acknowledge their cooperation: "Wedding in the Occupation," four pages within "White Boy Narrative," were based in part upon an interview Ron Grele conducted with Andrea Eagan (the bride) on February 18, 1985; "With SDSer Michael Balter at UCLA and in the Army" is based upon an interview that Ron Grele conducted with Michael Balter on January 3, 1985.

We have others to acknowledge, first those whose stories, kindly offered to us, that we were not able to use for scripts: Steve Fraser, Norm Diamond, Jay Jurie, and Jim Williams. Much gratitude goes to those whose stories we could use, gratitude for their patience with the complexities of the process and the inevitable condensation of personal narratives.

Thanks go, beyond the scope of the book proper, to the dozen graduate and undergraduate students in the Brown University spring 2007 class "The Sixties Without Apology," who undertook to prepare an exhibit based upon the comic images, with their own running commentary. And to the John Nicholas Brown Center, which hosted the opening exhibit and made the project possible. Steven Lubar and Chelsea Shriver in particular were immensely helpful.

We were encouraged from the beginning by Hill and Wang publisher Thomas LeBien. More than that: he proposed the idea, in no small part because a favorite aunt had been a leading figure in the Austin SDS branch. He has been hugely supportive, and patient, from start to finish.

Thanks to our artists, especially Gary Dumm, painstaking and devoted, one and all. Thanks to Harvey Pekar, scriptwriter extraordinaire who entered the project after it had been launched, and who added unimagined dimensions.

Special thanks also to George Kucewicz, former SDS rank and filer who encouraged the project from the beginning, and has been on board, in a variety of ways, all along.

And above all thanks to SDSers, past and present. This work properly belongs to you: it is your record, as well as we could record it in an emerging art form of the new century. Be yourselves and be proud.

211

ABOUT THE ARTISTS

Joshua Brown is executive director of the American Social History Project and professor of history at the Graduate Center, City University of New York. He is the author of *Beyond the Lines: Pictorial Reporting, Everyday Life, and the Crisis of Gilded Age America* (2002) and coauthor of *Forever Free: The Story of Emancipation and Reconstruction* (2005). His cartoons and illustrations regularly appear in print and online, including his weekly Web commentary on current politics, *Life During Wartime* (www.joshbrownnyc.com/ldw.htm).

James Cennamo is the staff cartoonist for *The Nantucket Independent*.

Gary Dumm has worked with Harvey Pekar on *American Splendor* since Pekar's self-publishing started thirty years ago, up to and including its current incarnation under the DC Comics (home of Superman and Batman) imprint. Currently, he writes and draws pieces for *Music Makers Rag* (biographies of blues musicians helped by that organization).

He has shown artwork in exhibitions nationally from Cleveland to San Francisco and internationally from Canada to Germany. His cartoons have been published in Cleveland's *Scene*, *Free Times*, and *Plain Dealer*, with appearances also in *Entertainment Weekly*, *The New York Times*, and France's *Le Monde*. A retrospective of his work was recently shown at the Artists Archives of the Western Reserve in Cleveland; simultaneously he exhibited several works in a show at San Francisco's Cartoon Museum called *Cartoon Tunes*. He contends that he will continue drawing comics and cartoons until they pry his weapon of choice (pencil, pen, brush, or marker) from his cold, dead hand.

Comic book artist **Summer McClinton** lives in New York City. She won the Xeric Award for her work on *THREAD*, a comic book novel by Emily Benz, and is now working on a long-form piece with Harvey Pekar. Her work has been described as "look[ing] nothing like a comic book."

Ed Piskor is a young cartoonist and principal artist of the forthcoming volume *The Beats*, scripted by Harvey Pekar. Visit him at www.edpiskor.com.

Nick Thorkelson's comics and cartoons include *The Underhanded History of the USA* (with Jim O'Brien), the "Econotoons" and "Comic Strip of Neoliberalism" features in *Dollars & Sense* magazine, and a regular series of cartoons on local politics for *The Boston Globe*. He got his start as a "movement cartoonist" illustrating the *ERAP Newsletter* in the summer of 1965.

Wes Modes is an illustrator, sculptor, community organizer, computer programmer, and train-hopper. He is a resident of Santa Cruz, California, and library system administrator at the University of California at Santa Cruz.

CPSIA information can be obtained
at www.ICGtesting.com
Printed in the USA
LVHW092217280819
629354LV00001B/80/P